Table of Cont

Introduction

C++ Succinctly was written to help professional C# developers learn modern C++ programming. The aim of this book is to leverage your existing C# knowledge in order to expand your skills. Whether you need to use C++ in an upcoming project, or simply want to learn a new language (or reacquaint yourself with it), this book will help you learn all of the fundamental pieces of C++ so you can understand projects and samples written in C++ and begin writing your own C++ programs.

As with any large subject, there simply wasn't room to cover everything (an example being the new atomic features added in C++11), and others might have decided to order the topics differently. I'm thinking particularly of pointers, a topic I cover in depth only further into the book. They are important, so some might have chosen to cover them earlier, but I feel you do not need to understand pointers to understand the material that precedes their coverage; understanding the preceding topics will make it much easier for you to understand them.

I've done my best to be as accurate as possible without sounding like a language specification or documentation file. I hope I have succeeded. I consulted the C++11 language specification frequently while writing this, and I also read everything from StackOverflow posts, to MSDN docs, to GCC docs, and beyond. There are areas where I intentionally simplified things. As you continue to expand your knowledge of C++, you will undoubtedly reach issues where you need to have a more comprehensive understanding in order to accomplish your goal or eliminate a bug. If reading this book imparts enough knowledge—and a good-enough feel for the language that you are able to recognize, diagnose, and resolve those issues—then I will be content that I have succeeded in my goals. Welcome to C++!

Preface

Trademarks, etc.

Being a retired lawyer, I feel compelled to include this brief section, which you probably don't care about unless you are a lawyer for one of these companies or organizations. The remainder of this preface is much more enjoyable reading for non-lawyers, so please don't let this put you off. Microsoft®, Visual Studio®, Visual C++®, Visual C#®, Windows®, Windows NT®, Win32®, MSDN®, Silverlight®, DirectX®, and IntelliSense® are registered trademarks of Microsoft Corporation. GNU® is a registered trademark of the Free Software Foundation. ISO® is a registered service mark of the International Organization for Standardization. IEC® is a registered service mark of International Engineering Consortium, Inc. Unicode® is a registered service mark of Unicode, Inc. (a.k.a. The Unicode Consortium). Intel® is a registered trademark of Intel Corporation. Other trademarks and service marks are the properties of their respective owners.

Program Entry Point

In C#, the entry point for a program is a static method named `Main`. Often you will not actually see it since various frameworks provide their own (e.g., Silverlight), but it is there, somewhere, since without it the operating system would not know where to begin executing your program.

The entry point of a C++ program is the `main` function. A simple version looks like this:

```cpp
int main(int argc, char* argv[])

{

    // Your program starts here.


    // Returning 0 signifies success.

    return 0;

}
```

The parameters are the argument count followed by an array of the command-line arguments (as strings). In Windows programming, you will often see this as the entry point:

```cpp
int wmain(int argc, wchar_t* argv[])

{

    // Your program starts here.


    // Returning 0 signifies success.

    return 0;

}
```

This `wmain` entry point is Microsoft-specific. It is used as the entry point for Windows Unicode programs (as opposed to older ASCII/code page programs). Microsoft operating systems that support Unicode (everything from Windows 2000 and Windows NT 4 on, and even Win 9X-based systems when you install a special add-on) use UTF-16 encoding. As such, you really should always use Unicode when writing your programs unless you absolutely need to support older systems that do not have Unicode support.

You will frequently also see this as the entry point for Windows programs:

```cpp
#include <tchar.h>


int _tmain(int argc, _TCHAR* argv[])
```

```
{
    // Your program starts here.


    // Returning 0 signifies success.

    return 0;
}
```

The Windows SDK provides the **tchar.h** header file, which you can (and should) use when you need to build a project that will be used on both Unicode and non-Unicode versions of Windows. I do not use it in the samples because, to the extent possible, I wanted to make the samples portable and standards-compliant.

Instead, I have written a small header file, **pchar.h**, which simplifies the entry-point portability issue. This does not solve most portability issues that crop up when dealing with strings; unfortunately, string portability is one area which simply isn't easy in C++. Indeed, my header file here is *not* a good example of what to do when you actually need the command-line arguments. We will discuss strings in much more detail later in the book. For now, first, here's the header file:

Sample: pchar.h

```
#pragma once


#if !defined(_PCHAR_H)

#define _PCHAR_H 1


#if defined(WIN32) && defined(UNICODE)

#define _pmain wmain

#define _pchar wchar_t

#else

#define _pmain main

#define _pchar char

#endif


#endif
```

Second, here's what the entry point now looks like (I have omitted the inclusion of the header file here):

```
int _pmain(int /*argc*/, _pchar* /*argv*/[])

{
```

```
// Your program starts here.


// Returning 0 signifies success.

return 0;
}
```

As you can see, the parameter names are commented out (using the C-style comment, i.e. /*...*/). This is perfectly legal in C++ and is something you should do whenever you have a function that is required to have certain parameters, although you may not intend to use those parameters. By commenting out the parameter names, you ensure that you will not accidentally use them.

The code in **pchar.h** gives us a reasonably portable entry point, while the `int _pmain(int, _pchar*[])` entry point itself ensures that we will never use the passed-in command-line arguments. If you ever need the command-line arguments, then this solution will not work—you will need a more advanced, more complicated solution.

Arguments and Parameters

I use the terms *argument* and *parameter* at various points in this book. To me, an argument is a value that is passed in to a function when called in a program, whereas a parameter is part of the specification of a function that tells the programmer the function is expecting to receive a value of a certain type. It also tells the programmer how it might treat that value. A parameter typically provides a name by which that value can be referenced, though C++ allows us to provide just a type if we are required to have a particular parameter (e.g., to match an interface specification) but do not intend to actually use its value.

As an example of a parameter versus an argument, in C# you might have a class method such as `void AddTwoNumbers(int a, int b, ref int result) { result = a + b; }`. In this case, `a`, `b`, and `result` are parameters; we know that `AddTwoNumbers` might change the value of the argument passed in for the `result` parameter (as, indeed, it does). If you called this method as so, `int one = 1, two = 2, answer = 0; someClass.AddTwoNumbers(one, two, ref answer);` then `one`, `two`, and `answer` would all be arguments passed in to `AddTwoNumbers`.

Syntax Highlighting

The code examples in this book use the syntax-highlighting colors from Visual Studio 2012 Ultimate RC. This will help you understand the code, but you will also be fine reading this on a monochrome e-book reader.

Samples

The samples in this book are available at
https://bitbucket.org/syncfusion/cpp_succinctly.

The samples for this book were designed and developed using Visual Studio 2012 Ultimate RC. The C++ compiler that comes with VS 2012 includes new features of the C++11 language standard that were not included in Visual Studio 2010. In the fall of 2012, Microsoft will release a free "Express" version of Visual Studio 2012, which will allow developers to use C++ targeted desktop applications (such as the console application, which the samples use). Until then, to make full use of the samples, you will need a non-Express version of Visual Studio 2012.

I tested many of the samples along the way using Minimalist GNU for Windows (MinGW), so there should be a lot of cross-compiler portability. The one sample I know for sure that does not work as written with the GCC compiler that MinGW provides is **StorageDurationSample**. It makes use of the Microsoft-specific language extension `_declspec(thread)` in order to simulate `thread_local` storage. GCC has its own very similar extension, and other compiler vendors undoubtedly do too, so if you replace that with the appropriate code for the compiler you decide to use, it should then compile and run.

Lastly, the samples are all console samples. I chose console samples so we could avoid all the extraneous code that comes with creating and displaying windows within a windowing environment. To see the output of any particular sample, you can either set a breakpoint on the `return` statement at the end of the `_pmain` function and then run it using the Visual Studio debugger, or you can run it using the **Start Without Debugging** command in the **Debug** menu in Visual Studio (typically this uses the Ctrl+F5 keyboard shortcut). You also need to make sure that the project you wish to run is set as the start-up project. You can accomplish this by right-clicking on the project's name in Solution Explorer and then left-clicking on **Set as Startup Project** in the context menu that appears.

C++11

In 2011, a new major version of the C++ language standard was adopted by the ISO/IEC working group responsible for the design and development of C++ as a language. When compared with C++98 and C++03, C++11 feels like a different language. Because C++11 is so new, there are no compilers that support every single feature, and there are some that support less than others. I have targeted Visual C++ and the features it implements in its most current release (Visual Studio 2012 RC at the time of this writing), though I have mentioned a few features that Visual C++ does not currently support and have pointed this out when appropriate.

It is unlikely that Visual C++ will change much between Visual Studio 2012 RC and Visual Studio 2012 RTM. There are plans to do an out-of-band update, which will add additional C++11 language support, sometime after the RTM is released. Since I cannot predict which features will be added and do not have any inside knowledge about it, I mostly did not cover things which are not supported in the RC.

If you have previous experience with C++ from five years ago, or perhaps longer, you are likely to be very pleasantly surprised—which is not to say that it has everything C# has.

There are features of C# and .NET that I miss when working in C++. But there are also features of C++ that I miss when working in C#. I miss the simplicity of casting in C# that the CLR's type system provides when I'm working in C++. I also miss .NET's fuller set of exceptions and the frequently better IntelliSense that .NET provides. In C++, I find myself referring to documentation a lot more than in C# to figure out things like what argument values I can and should pass to a particular function, and what values to expect back from it.

When I'm working in C#, I find myself missing the breadth that C++'s different storage durations provide. In C#, most things just wind up on the GC-managed heap, which greatly simplifies memory management. But sometimes I don't necessarily want a class instance to be on the heap. In C#, I have no choice but to rewrite the class as a structure; while in C++, I can easily choose between the two without needing to change the class definition itself. I also miss stand-alone functions (even though they can be mostly emulated with static methods in static classes in C#). I also like that my C++ programs end up as heavily optimized (and thus difficult to understand) machine code when I compile them, so I don't really need to worry about trying to obfuscate my programs if I want my code to stay secret (like I do with .NET, though there are some very good obfuscation tools out there).

Each language targets its own set of problems and has its own history and quirks associated with it. Hopefully you will find C++ an interesting and useful language to add to your programming repertoire.

Chapter 1   Types

Fundamental Types

C++ contains the same familiar keywords (e.g., int) that you recognize from C#. This is unsurprising given that both are C-like languages. There is, however, one potential landmine that can throw you into trouble. While C# explicitly defines the sizes of fundamental types (a short is a 16-bit integer, an int is a 32-bit integer, a long is a 64-bit integer, a double is a 64-bit double-precision IEEE 754 floating point number, etc.), C++ makes no such guarantees.

Implementations

Like many programming languages, there are multiple C++ implementations from various companies and organizations. Two of the most popular C++ implementations are Visual C++ and GCC. The C++ standard leaves some of its details to be defined by the implementer. If you are writing cross-platform code, you need to keep these implementation-defined details in mind, lest you find a program working fine on one OS and failing in weird ways on another.

The smallest fundamental unit in C++ is char, which only needs to be at least large enough to hold the 96 basic characters that the C++ standard specifies, plus any other characters in the implementation's basic character set. In theory, some implementation of C++ could define a char as 7 bits or 16 bits … almost anything is possible. But in practice you don't need to worry too much about a char being anything other than 8 bits (the equivalent of the byte or sbyte type in C#), which is its size in Visual C++.

In C++, char, signed char, and unsigned char are three distinct types. All three are required to take up the same amount of storage in memory. So a char in practice is either signed or unsigned. Whether it is signed or unsigned is implementation defined (see the sidebar). In Visual C++ the char type is, by default, signed. But you can use a compiler switch to have it treated as unsigned instead. In GCC, whether it is signed or unsigned depends on which CPU architecture you are targeting.

The signed integer types, in size order from smallest to largest, are:

1. signed char
2. short int
3. int
4. long int
5. long long int

The only guarantee of the size of each of these integer types is that each one is at least as large as the next smallest integer type. In Visual C++, an `int` and a `long int` are both 32-bit integers. It is only the `long long int` that is a 64-bit integer.

 Note: You can simply write `long` or `long long`; you do not need to write `long int` or `long long int`, respectively. The same is also true for `short int` (i.e. you can just write `short`). The `short` type is a 16-bit signed integer in Visual C++.

Each of the integer types has a corresponding unsigned integer type. You just put the keyword `unsigned` in front to get the unsigned version (except for `signed char`, which you change to `unsigned char`).

If you need to ensure that you are using specific sizes, you can include the C++ Standard Library header file **cstdint** (e.g., `#include <cstdint>`), which defines, among other things, the types:

- `int8_t`
- `int16_t`
- `int32_t`
- `int64_t`
- `uint8_t`
- `uint16_t`
- `uint32_t`
- `uint64_t`

These types have their use, but you will find that most APIs do not use them; instead, they use the fundamental types directly. This can make your programming confusing, as you constantly need to check the underlying fundamental type to ensure you do not end up with unintended truncation or expansion.

These types might come into use more, so I recommend checking for their usage in major libraries and APIs from time to time and adjusting your code accordingly if they become widely adopted. Of course, if you absolutely need a variable to be, for example, an unsigned 32-bit integer, you should certainly make use of `uint32_t` and make any adjustments for API calls and portability as needed.

Floating-point numbers are the same as far as size order rules. They go from `float` to `double` to `long double`. In Visual C++, `float` is a 32-bit floating-point number and `double` and `long double` are both 64-bit floating point numbers (`long double` is not larger than `double`, in other words).

C++ does not have any native type that is comparable to C#'s `decimal` type. However, one of the nice things about C++ is there are typically a large number of free or inexpensive libraries that you can license. For example, there's the decNumber library, the Intel Decimal Floating Point Math Library, and the GNU Multiple Precision Arithmetic Library. None are exactly compatible with C#'s decimal type, but if you are writing for Windows systems only, then you can use the DECIMAL data type to get that compatibility if needed, along with the Decimal Arithmetic Functions and the Data Type Conversion Functions.

There is also a Boolean type, `bool`, which can be `true` or `false`. In Visual C++, a `bool` takes up a byte. Unlike in C#, a `bool` can be transformed into an integer type. When false, it has an integer-equivalent value of 0, and when true, it has a value of 1. So the statement `bool result = true == 1;` will compile and `result` will evaluate to `true` when the statement has been executed.

Then there is the `wchar_t` type, which holds a wide character. A wide character's size varies based on the platform. On Windows platforms, it is a 16-bit character. It is the equivalent of C#'s `char` type. It is frequently used to construct strings. We will discuss strings in another chapter since many variants can be used for strings.

Lastly, there is the `void` type, which is used the same way it is in C#. And there is a `std::nullptr_t` type, which is messy to explain properly, but basically is there to be the type of the `nullptr` literal, which is what you should use instead of `NULL` or a literal `0` (zero) to check for null values.

Enumerations

Enumerations are fairly similar to each other in C++ and C#. C++ has two types of enums: scoped and un-scoped.

A scoped enumeration is defined as either an `enum class` or an `enum struct`. There is no difference between the two. An un-scoped enumeration is defined as a plain `enum`. Let's look at a sample:

Sample: EnumSample\EnumSample.cpp

```cpp
#include <iostream>
#include <ostream>
#include <string>
#include "../pchar.h"


enum class Color
{
    Red,
    Orange,
    Yellow,
    Blue,
    Indigo,
    Violet
};


// You can specify any underlying integral type you want, provided it fits.
enum Flavor : unsigned short int
{
    Vanilla,
    Chocolate,
    Strawberry,
    Mint,
};


int _pmain(int /*argc*/, _pchar* /*argv*/[])
{
    Flavor f = Vanilla;
```

```cpp
    f = Mint; // This is legal since the Flavor enum is an un-scoped enum.

    Color c = Color::Orange;

    //c = Orange; // This is illegal since the Color enum is a scoped enum.

    std::wstring flavor;

    std::wstring color;

    switch (c)
    {
    case Color::Red:
        color = L"Red";
        break;
    case Color::Orange:
        color = L"Orange";
        break;
    case Color::Yellow:
        color = L"Yellow";
        break;
    case Color::Blue:
        color = L"Blue";
        break;
    case Color::Indigo:
        color = L"Indigo";
        break;
    case Color::Violet:
        color = L"Violet";
        break;
    default:
        color = L"Unknown";
        break;
    }

    switch (f)
    {
```

```cpp
    case Vanilla:
            flavor = L"Vanilla";
            break;
    case Chocolate:
            flavor = L"Chocolate";
            break;
    case Strawberry:
            flavor = L"Strawberry";
            break;
    case Mint:
            flavor = L"Mint";
            break;
    default:
            break;
    }

    std::wcout << L"Flavor is " << flavor.c_str() << L" (" << f <<
            L"). Color is " << color.c_str() << L" (" <<
            static_cast<int>(c) << L")." << std::endl <<
            L"The size of Flavor is " << sizeof(Flavor) <<
            L"." << std::endl <<
            L"The size of Color is " << sizeof(Color) <<
            L"." << std::endl;

    return 0;
}
```

 Note: In C++, the scope resolution operator is ::. *We'll discuss this in more detail later on. For now, just think of it as serving many of the same purposes as the* . *operator in C#.*

This code will give the following output:

```
Flavor is Mint (3). Color is Orange (1).
The size of Flavor is 2.
The size of Color is 4.
```

As you can see in the sample, the scoped `Color` enumeration requires you to access its members in the same way as C# by prefacing the enumeration member with the enumeration's name and the scope resolution operator. By contrast, the un-scoped

`Flavor` enumeration allows you simply to specify the members without any prefix. For this reason, I think it's better practice to prefer scoped enumerations: You minimize the risks of naming collisions and lessen namespace pollution.

Notice that there is another difference with scoped enumerations: When we wanted to output the numerical value of the scoped `color` enum, we had to use the `static_cast` operator to convert it to an `int`, while we did not need to do any casting for the un-scoped `Flavor` enumeration.

For the `Flavor` enumeration, we specified the underlying type as being an unsigned short `int`. You can also specify the underlying type for scoped enumerations. Specifying the underlying type is optional, but is mandatory if you wish to use forward declaration with an un-scoped enumeration. Forward declaration is a way to speed up program compile times by only telling the compiler what it needs to know about a type rather than forcing it to compile the whole header file the type is defined in.

We will look at this later on. For now, just remember that an un-scoped enumeration must have its underlying type explicitly specified in order to use a forward declaration of it; a scope enumeration does not require specification of its underlying type to use a forward declaration of it (the underlying type will be `int` if none is specified).

You can do the same thing with enumerations in C++ as you can in C# in terms of explicitly assigning values to members, and in terms of creating flag enumerations. You do it all the same way, except you don't need to apply anything like the `FlagAttribute` in C++ to create flag enumerations; you just assign the correct values and proceed from there.

std::wcout, std::wcerr, std::wcin

The `std::wcout << L"Flavor`... code outputs wide character data to the standard output stream. In the case of a console program such as this, the standard output is the console window. There is also a `std::wcerr` output stream, which will output wide character data to the standard error output stream. This is also the console window, but you can redirect `std::wcout` output to one file and `std::wcerr` output to another file. There is also a `std::wcin` for inputting data from the console. We won't explore this, nor will we explore their byte counterparts: `std::cout`, `std::cerr`, and `std::cin`.

Just to let you see how the input looks, here's an example.

Sample: ConsoleSample\ConsoleSample.cpp

```cpp
#include <iostream>

#include <ostream>

#include <string>

#include "../pchar.h"


struct Color

{

    float ARGB[4];


    void A(float value) { ARGB[0] = value; }

    float A(void) const { return ARGB[0]; }

    void R(float value) { ARGB[1] = value; }

    float R(void) const { return ARGB[1]; }

    void G(float value) { ARGB[2] = value; }

    float G(void) const { return ARGB[2]; }

    void B(float value) { ARGB[3] = value; }

    float B(void) const { return ARGB[3]; }

};


// This is a stand-alone function, which happens to be a binary

// operator for the << operator when used with a wostream on

// the left and a Color instance on the right.

std::wostream& operator<<(std::wostream& stream, const Color& c)

{
```

```cpp
        stream << L"ARGB:{ " << c.A() << L"f, " << c.R() << L"f, " <<
            c.G() << L"f, " << c.B() << L"f }";

        return stream;
}


int _pmain(int /*argc*/, _pchar* /*argv*/[])
{
        std::wcout << L"Please input an integer and then press Enter: ";

        int a;


        std::wcin >> a;


        std::wcout << L"You entered '" << a << L"'." << std::endl;


        std::wcout << std::endl <<
            L"Please enter a noun (one word, no spaces) " <<
            L"and then press Enter: ";


        std::wstring noun;


        // wcin breaks up input using white space, so if you include a space or
        // a tab, then it would just put the first word into noun and there
        // would still be a second word waiting in the input buffer.
        std::wcin >> noun;


        std::wcerr << L"The " << noun << L" is on fire! Oh no!" << std::endl;


        Color c = { { 100.0f/255.0f, 149.0f/255.0f, 237.0f/255.0f, 1.0f } };


        // This uses our custom operator from above. Come back to this sample
        // later when we've covered operator overloading and this should make
        // much more sense.
        std::wcout << std::endl <<
            L"Cornflower Blue is " << c << L"." << std::endl;
```

```
        return 0;
}
```

The previous code is a fairly simple demo. It has no error checking, for instance. So, if you enter an incorrect value for the integer, it will just run through to the end with `std::wcin` returning instantly without any data (that's what it does unless and until you resolve the error).

If you are interested in iostream programming, including using things like `std::wofstream` to output data to a file and `std::wifstream` to read data in from a file (they work the same as `std::wcout` and `std::wcin`, just with added functionality for dealing with the fact that they work with files), see the MSDN iostream programming pages. Learning all the ins and outs of streams could easily fill a book just on its own.

One last thing though. You've undoubtedly noticed that the stream functionality looks a bit odd with the bit shifting operators << and >>. That's because these operators have been overloaded. While you would expect the bit shift operators to act a certain way on integers, there isn't any specific expectation you're likely to have about how they should work when applied to an output stream or an input stream, respectively. So the C++ Standard Library streams have co-opted these operators to use them for inputting and outputting data to streams. When we want the ability to read in or write out a custom type that we've created (such as the previous `color` structure), we simply need to create an appropriate operator overload. We'll learn more about operator overloading later in the book, so don't worry if it's a bit confusing right now.

Classes and Structures

The difference between a class and a structure in C++ is simply that a structure's members default to public whereas a class' members default to private. That's it. They are otherwise the same. There is no value-type versus reference-type distinction as there is in C#.

That said, typically you will see programmers use classes for elaborate types (combinations of data and functions) and structures for simple data-only types. Normally, this is a stylistic choice that represents the non-object-oriented origins of structure in C, making it easy to differentiate quickly between a simple data container versus a full-blown object by looking to see if it's a structure or a class. I recommend following this style.

 Note: An exception to this style is where a programmer is writing code that is meant to be used in both C and C++. Since C does not have a class type, the structure type might instead be used in ways similar to how you would use a class in C++. I'm not going to cover writing C-compatible C++ in this book. To do so, you would need to be familiar with the C language and the differences between it and C++. Instead, we are focusing on writing clean, modern C++ code.

In Windows Runtime ("WinRT") programming, a public structure can only have data members (no properties or functions). Those data members can only be made up of fundamental data types and other public structures—which, of course, have the same data-only, fundamental, and public-structures-only restrictions. Keep this in mind if you are working on any Metro-style apps for Windows 8 using C++.

You will sometimes see the `friend` keyword used within a class definition. It is followed by either a class name or a function declaration. What this code construct does is give that class or function access to the non-public member data and functions of the class. Typically, you'll want to avoid this since your class should normally expose everything you want to expose through its public interface. But in those rare instances where you do not wish to publicly expose certain data members or member functions, but do want one or more classes or functions to have access to it, you can use the `friend` keyword to accomplish this.

As classes are a very important part of C++ programming, we will explore them in much more detail later in the book.

Unions

The union type is a bit odd, but it has its uses. You will encounter it from time to time. A union is a data structure appearing to hold many data members, but only allowing you to use one of its data members at any one time. The end-result is a data structure that gives you many possible uses without wasting memory. The size of the union is required to be large enough only to contain the largest member of the union. In practice, this means the data members overlap each other in memory (hence, you can only use one at a time). This also means you have no way of knowing what the active member of a union is unless you keep track of it somehow. There are many ways you could do that, but putting a union and an enum in a structure is a good, simple, tidy way of doing it. Here's an example.

Sample: UnionSample\UnionSample.cpp

```cpp
#include <iostream>
#include <ostream>
#include "../pchar.h"


enum class SomeValueDataType
{
    Int = 0,
    Float = 1,
    Double = 2
};


struct SomeData
{
    SomeValueDataType Type;
    union
    {
        int iData;
        float fData;
        double dData;
    } Value;

    SomeData(void)
    {
```

```cpp
            SomeData(0);
    }

    SomeData(int i)
    {
        Type = SomeValueDataType::Int;

        Value.iData = i;
    }

    SomeData(float f)
    {
        Type = SomeValueDataType::Float;

        Value.fData = f;
    }

    SomeData(double d)
    {
        Type = SomeValueDataType::Double;

        Value.dData = d;
    }
};


int _pmain(int /*argc*/, _pchar* /*argv*/[])
{
    SomeData data = SomeData(2.3F);
    std::wcout << L"Size of SomeData::Value is " << sizeof(data.Value) <<
        L" bytes." << std::endl;


    switch (data.Type)
    {
    case SomeValueDataType::Int:
        std::wcout << L"Int data is " << data.Value.iData << L"."
            << std::endl;
        break;
    case SomeValueDataType::Float:
```

```
        std::wcout << L"Float data is " << data.Value.fData << L"F."

            << std::endl;

        break;

    case SomeValueDataType::Double:

        std::wcout << L"Double data is " << data.Value.dData << L"."

            << std::endl;

        break;

    default:

        std::wcout << L"Data type is unknown." << std::endl;

        break;

    }

    return 0;

}
```

As you can see, we define an enum that has members representing each of the types of members of the union. We then define a structure that includes both a variable of the type of that enum and then an anonymous union. This gives us all the information we need to determine which type the union is currently holding within one encapsulated package.

If you wanted the union to be usable in multiple structures, you could declare it outside of the structure and give it a name (e.g., `union SomeValue { ... };`). You could then use it within the structure as, for example, `SomeValue Value;`. It's usually better to keep it as an anonymous union though, since you do not need to worry about the side effects of making a change except within the structures in which it is defined.

Unions can have constructors, destructors, and member functions. But since they can have only one active data member ever, it rarely makes any sense to write member functions for a union. You will rarely see them, perhaps never.

typedef

The first thing to understand about `typedef` is that despite the implications of its name, `typedef` does not create new types. It is an aliasing mechanism that can be used for many things.

It is used a lot in implementing the C++ Standard Library and other template-based code. This is, arguably, its most important use. We will explore it more in the chapter on templates.

It can save you from a lot of typing (though this argument lost some of its force with the repurposing of the `auto` keyword for type deduction in C++11). If you have a particularly complicated data type, creating a `typedef` for it means you only need to type it out once. If your complicated data type's purpose is unclear, giving it a more semantically meaningful name with a `typedef` can help make your program easier to understand.

It is sometimes used as an abstraction by developers to easily change a backing type (e.g., from a `std::vector` to a `std::list`) or the type of a parameter (e.g., from an `int` to a `long`). For your own internal-use-only code, this should be frowned upon. If you are developing code that others will be using, such as a library, you should never try to use a `typedef` in this way. All you are doing is decreasing the discoverability of breaking changes to your API if you change a `typedef`. Use them to add semantic context, sure, but do not use them to change an underlying type in code that others rely on.

If you need to change the type of something, remember that any change to a function's parameters is a breaking change as is a change in return type or the addition of a default argument. The proper way to handle the possibility of a future type change is with abstract classes or with templates (whichever is more suitable or whichever you prefer, if both will serve). This way the public interface to your code will not change, only the implementation will. The Pimpl idiom is another good way to keep a stable API while retaining the freedom to change implementation details. We will explore the Pimpl idiom, short for "pointer to implementation," in a later chapter.

Here is a small code block illustrating the syntax for `typedef`.

```
class ExistingType;


typedef ExistingType AliasForExistingType;
```

And the following is a brief sample showing how `typedef` might be used. The purpose of this sample is to illustrate a simplified but realistic use of a `typedef`. In practice, a `typedef` like this would go into a namespace and would then be included in a header file. Since we haven't covered any of that, this example has been kept simple intentionally.

Sample: TypedefSample\TypedefSample.cpp

```cpp
#include <iostream>
#include <ostream>
#include <vector>
#include <algorithm>
#include "../pchar.h"


// This makes WidgetIdVector an alias for std::vector<int>, which has
// more meaning than std::vector<int> would have, since now we know that
// anything using this alias expects a vector of widget IDs
// rather than a vector of integers.
typedef std::vector<int> WidgetIdVector;


bool ContainsWidgetId(WidgetIdVector idVector, int id)
{
    return (std::end(idVector) !=
        std::find(std::begin(idVector), std::end(idVector), id)
        );
}


int _pmain(int /*argc*/, _pchar* /*argv*/[])
{
    WidgetIdVector idVector;

    // Add some id numbers to the vector.
    idVector.push_back(5);
    idVector.push_back(8);

    // Output a result letting us know if the id is in the
    // WidgetIdVector.
    std::wcout << L"Contains 8: " <<
        (ContainsWidgetId(idVector, 8) ? L"true." : L"false.") <<
        std::endl;

    return 0;
}
```

Chapter 2   Namespaces

The Global Namespace

Consider the following code:

Sample: GlobalNamespaceSample\GlobalNamespaceSample.cpp

```cpp
#include <iostream>
#include <ostream>
#include "../pchar.h"


int g_x = 10;


int AddTwoNumbers(int a, int b)
{
    return a + b;
}


int _pmain(int /*argc*/, _pchar* /*argv*/[])
{
    int y = 20;
    std::wcout << L"The result of AddTwoNumbers(g_x, y) where g_x = " <<
        g_x << L" and y = " << y << L" is " << AddTwoNumbers(g_x, y) <<
        L"." << std::endl;

    if (true == 1)
    {
        std::wcout << L"true == 1!" << std::endl;
    }
    return 0;
}
```

C++ lets you have methods that are not part of a class. These are called functions. More particularly, they are often called stand-alone functions since the C++ terminology for a class method is a class member function. We will discuss functions in much more detail in a later chapter.

In the previous sample, we define two functions, `AddTwoNumbers` and `wmain`. These two functions are both in the global namespace. The global namespace is the base level in which everything else within the program exists. C++, owing to its C heritage, allows you to define anything within the global namespace (so you can define namespaces, classes, structures, variables, functions, enums, and templates).

C# also has the concept of a global namespace, but it does not allow you to define anything within it other than namespaces and types. In the previous example, we have the statement `int g_x = 10;` which defines an integer named g_x within the global namespace and assigns it a value of 10. This is what is commonly referred to as a global variable. In C# global variables are illegal.

As a brief aside, every programming language I have ever worked with has had its share of bad features—things the language allows, but things that usually lead to issues. These issues include hard-to-debug problems, subtle errors that go unnoticed for a long time, maintainability problems, readability problems, and all the other frustrating things that add many hours to development time without any benefit. C++ is no different. When we come across something that fits this description, I will do my best to call it out. This is one of those times.

Global variables are bad. Avoid them whenever possible. There is a common convention when using them in C++, which is to prefix the variable name with `g_`, as in the previous example. While this helps to alert you and other programmers to the fact that this is a global variable, it does not change the fact that it is a global variable, having all the problems I described. This isn't a book on bad programming practices, so I'm not going to spend time explaining why global variables are bad. All you need to know is this feature exists in C++, but you should avoid using it whenever possible.

The Scope Resolution Operator ':::'

In C++, :: is the scope resolution operator. It is used for separating nested namespaces, for separating types from their namespace, and for separating member functions and variables from their type.

Note that it is only used in the last situation when performing the following:

- Defining a member function.
- Accessing a member of a base class within a member function definition.
- Accessing a static member function or variable.
- Assigning a value to a static member variable.
- Fetching the address of a member function.

In other instances, you use either the . operator or the -> operator, depending on whether you are accessing the member directly or via a pointer.

This can seem complicated since C# just uses the . operator for all of the purposes that ::, ., and -> are used for in C++.

 Note: We'll discuss the . and -> operators later. For now, you just need to know that they are used for accessing instance member variables and non-static member functions (which you use depending on whether or not you are working with a pointer).

For the most part, you'll be fine. The only place you're likely to trip up is if you try to access a base class member by using the . operator rather than the :: operator, or if you try to specify an enum member using something other than ::. If you ever compile your program and receive a syntax error complaining about "missing ';' before '.' ", it's a good bet you used a . where you should've used a :: instead.

Defining Namespaces

A namespace is defined in much the same way as it is in C#. Here is an example:

Sample: NamespacesSample\NamespacesSample.cpp

```cpp
#include <iostream>
#include <ostream>
#include <string>
#include "../pchar.h"


using namespace std;


namespace Places
{
    namespace Cities
    {
        struct City
        {
            City(const wchar_t* name)
            {
                Name = wstring(name);
            }


            wstring Name;
        };
    }
}


int _pmain(int /*argc*/, _pchar* /*argv*/[])
{
    auto nyc = Places::Cities::City(L"New York City");


    wcout << L"City name is " << nyc.Name.c_str() << L"." << endl;


    return 0;
}
```

As you can see, we can nest namespaces and in turn access those namespaces and the types contained within them using the scope resolution operator. You'll also notice that we used the `auto` keyword. This is the C++ equivalent of C#'s `var` keyword.

The using namespace Directive

Looking at the **NamespacesSample**, notice that we've included the line `using namespace std;`. This line looks very similar to the `using` directive in C#, and it is; however, in C# the `using` directive automatically brings into scope any types in that namespace which are in any of the referenced assemblies. By contrast, in C++ a `using` directive only brings into scope the types in the included header files, not all of the types in the libraries that will be linked to your program or library. What are header files you ask? That question provides a good segue into the next chapter.

 Note: Never include a using directive in a header file. If you do that, you don't just import the types and namespaces in that namespace into the header file, you also import them into any source or header file that includes the header file. This causes really nasty namespace pollution issues. We'll be discussing header files next, so anything that's unclear about this should make sense then. Just remember that having a `using namespace` *directive in a header file is a bad idea; only use them in your source code files.*

Chapter 3   Functions and Classes

Declaration vs. Definition

 Tip: This first section, "Declaration vs. Definition," is a bit dense. Understanding these concepts before looking at a sample will help you understand the sample. In turn, looking at a sample will help you understand these concepts. I recommend you read this and then look through the samples in the next two sections. If parts of this section weren't clear, come back to reread this section.

In C#, classes and other types are declared and defined at the same time. Even with the `partial` keyword, the class definition is simply allowed to spread over multiple files; it does not change the combination of declaration and definition. The only exception to this rule is when doing interop (which uses `DllImportAttribute` and the `extern` keyword to declare a function defined in an external DLL). In that case, the definition isn't in C# but is almost certainly in some non-.NET library. (If the DLL was a .NET assembly, you could just add a reference to it and use it without any interop code being necessary.)

I write this because in C++, declaration and definition can usually be separated, and frequently are. It is common to see a class declared in a header file (which, by convention, has a .H suffix) and defined in a source file (which, by convention, has a .CPP suffix). This is true not just for classes, but also for stand-alone functions and even structures and unions when they have member functions associated with them.

Expect to see one or more `#include "SomeHeader.h"` lines at the top of a .CPP file. These statements tell the compiler (or, more accurately, the preprocessor) that there are declarations and possibly definitions in that file, or in files included from it, that are necessary for the compiler to make sense of parts of the C++ code that follows.

With Visual C++, when including a header that is part of your project or is not found in the build system's include path, use the `#include "HeaderFile.h"` syntax. When including a system include file, such as Windows.h, use the `#include <Windows.h>` syntax. Lastly, when including an include file that is part of the C++ Standard Library (which we will discuss in more detail later), use the `#include <vector>` syntax (i.e. no .h is included). The meaning of the " " versus the < > syntax for including files is implementation-defined, though both GCC and Visual C++ use quoted syntax for local header files and bracketed syntax for system header files.

 Note: The reason the .H suffix was left off from the C++ Standard Library include files was to avoid naming collisions with C++ compilers that already provided header files that used those names when the C++ Standard Library was introduced. They are normal header files, have no fear.

To understand why the difference between declaration and definition matters in C++, it's important to have a basic understanding of the C++ build process. Here's what generally happens:

1. The preprocessor examines a source file, inserts the text of the files specified by the include statements (and the text of the files specified by their include statements, etc.), and also evaluates and acts on any other preprocessor directives (e.g., expanding macros) and any pragma directives.

2. The compiler takes the output from the preprocessor and compiles that code into machine code, which it stores, along with other information needed for the linking phase, in an OBJ file.

3. Steps 1 and 2 are repeated for each source file within the project.

4. The linker examines the output files from the compiler and the library files that your project links. It finds all of the places where the compiler identified something as being declared but not defined within that particular source file. It then locates the appropriate address for the definition and patches that address in.

5. Once everything has been linked successfully, the linker binds everything together and outputs the finished product (typically either an executable program or a library file).

An error during any of those phases will stop the build process, of course, and the previous description is only a rough sketch of the Visual C++ build chain. Compiler authors have some flexibility in exactly how they do things. For example, there's no requirement that any intermediate files be produced, so in theory, the whole build process could be done in memory, though in practice, I doubt anyone would ever do that. So consider that list as just a rough outline, not an exact description.

I've been referring to everything as source files to keep the terminology simple. Within the C++ standard, these combinations of a source file plus all of its include files is referred to as a compilation unit. I mention that now only because I will be using the term a bit further along. Let's consider the three build phases in turn.

The preprocessor doesn't care about C++ declarations and definitions. Indeed, it doesn't even care if your program is in C++. The only business it has with your source files is to take care of all lines that begin with a #, thus marking them as preprocessor directives. As long as those lines are properly formed, and it can find all of the included files, if any, the preprocessor will do its work, adding and removing text as directed. It will pass the results on to the compiler, typically without writing its result out to a file since compilation immediately follows preprocessing.

The compiler does care about declarations and definitions and very much is concerned with whether your program is valid C++ code or not. However, it doesn't need to know what a function does when it comes across it. It just needs to know what the function signature is—such as int `AddTwoNumbers(int, int)`;.

The same is true for classes, structures, and unions; as long as the compiler knows the declaration (or in the case of a pointer, simply that the particular token is a class, a structure, a union, or an enum), then it doesn't need any definitions. With just the declaration, it knows if your call to `AddTwoNumbers` is syntactically correct and that the class `Vehicle;` is in fact a class, so it can create a pointer to it when it sees `Vehicle* v;`, which is all it cares about.

The linker does care about definitions. Specifically, it cares that there is one, and only one, definition matching each of the declarations in your project. The lone exception is inline functions, which end up being created in each compilation unit in which they are used. However, they are created in a way that avoids any issues with multiple definitions.

You can have duplicate declarations among the compilation units for your program; doing so is a common trick for improving build times, as long as only one definition matches a declaration (except for inlines). In order to ensure this one definition rule is met, C++ compilers tend to use something called name mangling.

This ensures each declaration is matched up with its proper definition, including issues such as overloaded functions and namespaces (which allow the same name to be reused if the uses are in different namespaces), and class, structure, union, and enum definitions nested within classes, structures, or unions.

This name mangling is what results in terrifying linker errors, which we will see an example of in the "Inline Member Functions" section.

The severability of declarations from definitions lets you build your C++ projects without recompiling each source file every time. It also lets you build projects that use libraries for which you do not have the source code. There are, of course, other ways to accomplish those goals (C# uses a different build process for instance). This is the way C++ does it; understanding that basic flow helps make sense of many peculiarities in C++ that you do not encounter in C#.

Functions

There are two types of functions in C++: stand-alone functions and member functions. The main difference between them is that a member function belongs to a class, structure, or union, whereas a stand-alone function does not.

Stand-alone functions are the most basic types of functions. They can be declared in namespaces, they can be overloaded, and they can be inline. Let's look at a few.

Sample: FunctionsSample\Utility.h

```cpp
#pragma once


namespace Utility
{
    inline bool IsEven(int value)
    {
        return (value % 2) == 0;
    }


    inline bool IsEven(long long value)
    {
        return (value % 2) == 0;
    }


    void PrintIsEvenResult(int value);
    void PrintIsEvenResult(long long value);


    void PrintBool(bool value);
}
```

Sample: FunctionsSample\Utility.cpp

```cpp
#include "Utility.h"
#include <iostream>
#include <ostream>


using namespace std;
using namespace Utility;
```

```cpp
void Utility::PrintIsEvenResult(int value)
{
    wcout << L"The number " << value << L" is " <<
        (IsEven(value) ? L"" : L"not ") << L"even."
        << endl;
}


void Utility::PrintIsEvenResult(long long value)
{
    wcout << L"The number " << value << L" is " <<
        (IsEven(value) ? L"" : L"not ") << L"even."
        << endl;
}


void Utility::PrintBool(bool value)
{
    wcout << L"The value is" <<
        (value ? L"true." : L"false.") << endl;
}
```

Sample: FunctionsSample\FunctionsSample.cpp

```cpp
#include "Utility.h"
#include "../pchar.h"


using namespace Utility;


int _pmain(int /*argc*/, _pchar* /*argv*/[])
{
    int i1 = 3;
    int i2 = 4;


    long long ll1 = 6;
    long long ll2 = 7;


    bool b1 = IsEven(i1);
```

```
    PrintBool(b1);


    PrintIsEvenResult(i1);

    PrintIsEvenResult(i2);

    PrintIsEvenResult(l11);

    PrintIsEvenResult(l12);



    return 0;

}
```

The header file **Utility.h** declares and defines two inline functions, both called `IsEven` (making `IsEven` an overloaded function). It also declares three more functions: two called `PrintIsEvenResult` and one called `PrintBool`. The source file **Utility.cpp** defines these last three functions. Lastly, the source file **FunctionsSample.cpp** uses that code to create a simple program.

Any functions defined in a header file must be declared inline; otherwise, you'll wind up with multiple definitions and a linker error. Also, function overloads need to be different by more than just their return type; otherwise, the compiler cannot make sure you are really getting the version of the method you wanted. C# is the same way, so this shouldn't be anything new.

As seen in **Utility.cpp**, when you are defining a stand-alone function that is in a namespace, you need to put the namespace before the function name and separate it with the scope resolution operator. If you used nested namespaces, you include the whole namespace nesting chain—for example, `void`

`RootSpace::SubSpace::SubSubSpace::FunctionName(int param) { ... };`.

Simple Class

The following sample includes a class broken into a header file and a source file.

Sample: SimpleClassSample\VehicleCondition.h

```cpp
#pragma once
#include <string>


namespace Inventory
{

    enum class VehicleCondition
    {
        Excellent = 1,
        Good = 2,
        Fair = 3,
        Poor = 4
    };


    inline const std::wstring GetVehicleConditionString(
        VehicleCondition condition
        )
    {

    std::wstring conditionString;

    switch (condition)
    {
    case Inventory::VehicleCondition::Excellent:
        conditionString = L"Excellent";
        break;
    case Inventory::VehicleCondition::Good:
        conditionString = L"Good";
        break;
    case Inventory::VehicleCondition::Fair:
        conditionString = L"Fair";
        break;
    case Inventory::VehicleCondition::Poor:
```

```cpp
                    conditionString = L"Poor";

                    break;

            default:

                    conditionString = L"Unknown Condition";

                    break;

            }


            return conditionString;

    }

}
```

Sample: SimpleClassSample\Vehicle.h

```cpp
#pragma once

#include <string>


namespace Inventory

{

    enum class VehicleCondition;


    class Vehicle

    {

    public:

        Vehicle(

                VehicleCondition condition,

                double pricePaid

                );


        ~Vehicle(void);


        VehicleCondition GetVehicleCondition(void)

        {

            return m_condition;

        };


        void SetVehicleCondition(VehicleCondition condition);
```

```cpp
        double GetBasis(void) { return m_basis; };


    private:

        VehicleCondition        m_condition;

        double                  m_basis;

    };

}
```

Sample: SimpleClassSample\Vehicle.cpp

```cpp
#include "Vehicle.h"

#include "VehicleCondition.h"


using namespace Inventory;

using namespace std;


Vehicle::Vehicle(VehicleCondition condition, double pricePaid) :

    m_condition(condition),

    m_basis(pricePaid)

{

}


Vehicle::~Vehicle(void)

{

}


void Vehicle::SetVehicleCondition(VehicleCondition condition)

{

    m_condition = condition;

}
```

Sample: SimpleClassSample\SimpleClassSample.cpp

```cpp
#include <iostream>

#include <ostream>

#include <string>

#include <iomanip>

#include "Vehicle.h"
```

```
#include "VehicleCondition.h"

#include "../pchar.h"


using namespace Inventory;

using namespace std;


int _pmain(int /*argc*/, _pchar* /*argv*/[])

{

    auto vehicle = Vehicle(VehicleCondition::Excellent, 325844942.65);

    auto condition = vehicle.GetVehicleCondition();

    wcout << L"The vehicle is in " <<

        GetVehicleConditionString(condition).c_str() <<

        L" condition. Its basis is $" << setw(10) <<

        setprecision(2) << setiosflags(ios::fixed) <<

        vehicle.GetBasis() << L"." << endl;


    return 0;

}
```

In **Vehicle.h**, we begin with a forward declaration of the vehicleCondition enum class. We will discuss this technique more at the end of the chapter. For now the key points are (1) that we could either use this forward declaration or include the **VehicleCondition.h** header file and (2) that the declaration of vehicleCondition must come before the class definition for vehicle.

In order for the compiler to allot enough space for instances of vehicle, it needs to know how large each data member of vehicle is. We can let it know either by including the appropriate header file or, in certain circumstances, by using a forward declaration. If the declaration of vehicleCondition came after the definition of vehicle, then the compiler would refuse to compile the code since the complier would not know how big vehicleCondition is or even what type of data it is.

In that case, a simple declaration suffices to tell the compiler what vehicleCondition is (an enum class) and how big it is. Enum classes default to using an int as their backing field unless otherwise specified. If we leave the backing field blank, but then say to use a short, or a long, or some other backing field type somewhere else, the compiler would generate a different error message, telling us we have multiple, conflicting declarations.

We then proceed to define the vehicle class. The definition includes the declaration of its member functions and its member variables. For the most part, we do not define the member functions. The exceptions are the GetVehicleCondition member function and the GetBasis member function, which we will discuss in the "Inline Member Functions" section.

We define the other member functions of Vehicle in **Vehicle.cpp**. In this case, the member functions are the constructor, the destructor, and SetVehicleCondition. Typically, a function like SetVehicleCondition would be inline, so would simple constructors and destructors in the Vehicle class. They are defined separately here to illustrate how you define these types of member functions when they are not inline functions. We will discuss the odd-looking constructor syntax in the chapter devoted to constructors. The rest of the Vehicle class code should be clear.

 Note: Although you are not required to adopt the ClassName.h or ClassName.cpp file naming convention, you will see it in use almost everywhere because it makes using and maintaining code easier.

The GetVehicleConditionString inline function in **VehicleCondition.h** returns a copy of the std::wstring created in that function, not the local value itself. Coming from C#, you might think this a bit odd without having a new keyword used. We will explore this when we discuss the automatic duration type in the chapter on storage duration.

The entry point function uses some of the C++ Standard Library's I/O formatting functionality.

Member Functions

As discussed earlier, member functions are part of a class, structure, or union. Simply, I will talk about them as class members from here on.

Static member functions can call other static class member functions, regardless of protection level. Static member functions can also access static class member data either explicitly (i.e. `SomeClass::SomeFloat = 20.0f;`) or implicitly (i.e. `SomeFloat = 20.0f;`), regardless of protection level.

The explicit form is helpful if you have a parameter with the same name as a class member. Prefixing member data with an `m_`, such as `m_SomeFloat`, eliminates that problem and makes it clear when you are working with class member data versus local variables or parameters. That's just a style choice, not a requirement.

Instance (i.e. non-static) member functions are automatically assigned a `this` pointer to the instance data for the instance on which they were called. Instance member functions can call other class member functions and access all class member data either explicitly—the same as static members using `this->m_count++;` for instance data —or implicitly—the same as static and instance data (e.g., `m_data++;`), regardless of protection level.

Inline Member Functions

In **SampleClass\Vehicle.h**, the `GetVehicleCondition` and `GetBasis` member functions are both declared and defined. This combination of declaration and definition is called an inline member function in C++. Since this is similar to writing methods in C#, it might be inviting to do so in C++ as well. With some exceptions, you shouldn't do this.

As we discussed previously, when you build a C++ project, the compiler goes through each of your source files only once. It may make many passes at the same source files to optimize them, but it's not going to come back again after it is finished.

In contrast, the compiler will come back to your header files every time they are included in another file, regardless of whether it's a source file or another header file. This means the compiler can end up running through the code in the header files many, many times during a build.

At the beginning of the **SampleClass\Vehicle.h** header file, you see the `#pragma once` directive. This is a useful and important line. If you include the header file **A.h** in a source file and then include another header file that has **A.h**, the `#pragma once` directive would tell the preprocessor not to include the contents of **A.h** again. This prevents the preprocessor from bouncing back and forth between two header files that include each other indefinitely. It also prevents compiler errors. If **A.h** was included multiple times, the compiler would fail when it reached a type definition from the second inclusion of **A.h**.

Even with that directive, the compiler still needs to include and parse that header file code for each source file that includes it. The more things you put into your header file, the longer it takes to build each source file. This increases compilation time, which, as you will discover, can be quite lengthy with C++ projects when compared with C#.

When you do include a member function's definition inline in the header file, the C++ compiler can make that code inline in any source file where that function is used. This typically results in faster program executions since, rather than needing to make a call to a function, the program can simply run the code in place.

Scope is preserved by the compiler, so you don't need to worry about naming collisions between variables defined in the inline function and in a function where it is used. When dealing with code, such as the previous examples, where you are simply retrieving a member variable's value, inline definitions can improve speed, especially if the code is executing within a loop.

There is an alternate way to define an inline member function. If you want to keep your class definitions nice and clean, with no member function definitions within

them, but still want to have some inline member functions, you can do something like
the following instead:

**Sample: SimpleClassSample\Vehicle.h (alternate code commented out at the
bottom of the file).**

```cpp
#pragma once

#include <string>


namespace Inventory

{

    enum class VehicleCondition;


    class Vehicle

    {

    public:

        Vehicle(

            VehicleCondition condition,

            double pricePaid

            );


        ~Vehicle(void);


        inline VehicleCondition GetVehicleCondition(void);


        void SetVehicleCondition(VehicleCondition condition);


        inline double GetBasis(void);


    private:

        VehicleCondition        m_condition;

        double                  m_basis;

    };


    VehicleCondition Vehicle::GetVehicleCondition(void)

    {

        return m_condition;
```

```
       }


double Vehicle::GetBasis(void)

{

        return m_basis;

    }

}
```

As you can see, after the class declaration, we defined the member functions we
wanted inline, just as we would if they were in a source file. The key difference is
that the function declarations in the class are preceded by the `inline` keyword, and the
function definitions are in the header file itself. If you leave that keyword off, you
will get a linker error as in Figure 1.

*Figure 1: The result of leaving the `inline` keyword
off of the `Vehicle::GetVehicleCondition` member function.*

Linker errors are always horrible looking, by the way. The reason is that the linker no
longer knows what your variables and functions were named in the source file. It
only knows what the compiler transformed those names into in order to make all the
names unique. This includes overload methods, which need a unique name at the
linking stage so the linker can connect a call to an overloaded member function to the
correct overload version of that function.

The errors in Figure 1 are simply telling us that we defined
`Inventory::Vehicle::GetVehicleCondition(void)` more than once. Now, we know we only
defined it once, just in the header file, but we have included the header file in both
Vehicle.cpp and in **Main.cpp** in the **SimpleClassSample** project.

Since we intentionally *forgot* to add the `inline` keyword to the
`Vehicle::GetVehicleCondition` function declaration, the compiler doesn't make the code
inline. Instead, it compiles it as a function in both **Main.cpp** and **Vehicle.cpp**.

This, of course, is something the compiler is fine with because it treats each source file as a unique compilation unit. The compiler doesn't know any better, since, by the time the code reaches it, the code has already been inserted by the preprocessor stage. Only when the linker gets all the compiled code and tries to match everything up do we reach a phase where the build process says, "Hey, I already have another version of this function!" and then fails.

As you can see, there are two ways of making member functions inline. Both must be done within the header file since the compiler will evaluate the header-file code as many times as they are included, but it will only run through source files once. If you use the second method and forget an `inline` keyword, then you will have horrible linker errors. If you use the second method and remember the `inline` keyword, but define the functions within the source file, you will get horrible linker errors—this time saying there is no definition.

 Tip: Don't try to make everything inline. You will just end up with slow compile times that kill your productivity. Do inline things that make sense, like simple getter and setter functions for member variables. Like anything else, profile first, and then optimize if needed.

Protection Levels and Access Specifiers

Member functions and member data have three possible access specifiers:

- `public`
- `protected`
- `private`

These access specifiers denote the level of accessibility that the member has. In **SampleClass\Vehicle.h**, you can see two examples of how these are used. Note that unlike in C#, you do not restate the access specifier in front of each member. Instead, you state the access specifier, followed by a colon (e.g., `public:`), and then every declaration and definition that comes after is given that level of accessibility until you reach another access specifier.

By default, class members are private. This means if you have no access specifier at the beginning of the class declaration, then all members that are declared will be private until an access specifier is reached. If none is reached, you'd have an entirely private class, which would be very odd.

Structure members default to public, so on occasion you'll see a structure without any access specifiers. If you wish to use them in a structure, though, they work the same as in a class.

Lastly, you can use the same access specifier more than once; if you want to organize your class so you define the member functions first and then the member variables (or vice versa), you could easily do something like this:

> *Note: This code is expository only; it is not included in any of the samples.*

```
#include <string>


class SomeClass

{

public:

    SomeClass(void);

    virtual ~SomeClass(void);

    int AddTwoInts(int, int);

    void StoreAString(const wchar_t*);

private:

    bool CheckForIntAdditionOverflow(int, int);

public:
```

```
    int        SomePublicInteger;
protected:

    std::wstring    m_storedString;
};
```

The previous class definition doesn't define anything particularly useful. However, it does serve as an example of the use of all three access specifiers. It also demonstrates that you can use specifiers more than once, such as `public` in the previous example.

Inheritance

When specifying classes that your class derives from In C++, you should also specify an access specifier. If not, you will get the default access levels: private for a class and public for a structure. Note that I said classes. C++ supports multiple-inheritance. This means a class or structure can have more than one direct base class or structure, unlike C# where a class can have only one parent.

C++ does not have a separate interface type. In general, multiple-inheritance should be avoided except as a workaround for lack of a separate interface. In other words, a class should have only zero or one real base class along with zero or more purely abstract classes (interfaces). This is just a personal style recommendation, though.

There are some good arguments for multiple-inheritance. For instance, say you have three groups of functionality. Each one consists of functions and data. Then say each group is unrelated to the other—there's no connection between them, but they aren't mutually exclusive. In this case, you may wish to put each functionality group into its own class. Then if you have a situation where you want to create a class needing two of these groups, or even all three, you can simply create a class that inherits from all three, and you're done.

Or, you're done as long as you didn't have any naming conflicts in your public and protected members' functions and variables. For example, what if all three of the functionality groups have a member function `void PrintDiagnostics(void);`? You'd be doomed, *yes*? Well, it turns out that *no*, you are not doomed (usually). You need to use some weird syntax to specify which base class' `PrintDiagnostics` function you want. And even then you aren't quite done.

C++ lets you specify whether you want a class to be a plain base class or a virtual base class. You do this by putting or not putting the keyword `virtual` before the class' name in the base class specifier. We'll look at a sample shortly that addresses all of this, but before we do, it's important to understand that if you inherit a class at least twice, and two or more of the inheritance's are not virtual, you will end up with multiple copies of that class' data members

This causes a whole bunch of problems when trying to specify which of those you wish to use. Seemingly, the solution is to derive from everything virtually, but that has a run-time performance hit associated with it due to how C++ implementations tend to resolve virtual members. Better still, try to avoid having this ever happen in the first place, but as that's not always possible, do remember virtual inheritance.

And now a sample to help make this all make sense:

Sample: InheritanceSample\InheritanceSample.cpp

```
#include <iostream>
```

```cpp
#include <ostream>
#include <string>
#include <typeinfo>
#include "../pchar.h"

using namespace std;

class A
{
public:
    A(void) : SomeInt(0) { }

    virtual ~A(void) { }

    const wchar_t* Id(void) const { return L"A"; }

    virtual const wchar_t* VirtId(void) const { return L"A"; }

    int GetSomeInt(void) const { return SomeInt; }

    int             SomeInt;
};

class B1 : virtual public A
{
public:
    B1(void) :
        A(),
        m_fValue(10.0f)
    {
        // Because SomeInt isn't a member of B, we
        // cannot initialize it in the initializer list
        // before the open brace where we initialize the
        // A base class and the m_fValue member data.
        SomeInt = 10;
    }
```

```cpp
        virtual ~B1(void) { }

        const wchar_t* Id(void) const { return L"B1"; }

        virtual const wchar_t* VirtId(void) const override
        {
            return L"B1";
        }

        const wchar_t* Conflict(void) const { return L"B1::Conflict()"; }

private:
        float           m_fValue;
};

class B2 : virtual public A
{
public:
        B2(void) : A() { }
        virtual ~B2(void) { }

        const wchar_t* Id(void) const { return L"B2"; }

        virtual const wchar_t* VirtId(void) const override
        {
            return L"B2";
        }

        const wchar_t* Conflict(void) const { return L"B2::Conflict()"; }

};

class B3 : public A
{
public:
```

```cpp
        B3(void) : A() { }
        virtual ~B3(void) { }

        const wchar_t* Id(void) const { return L"B3"; }

        virtual const wchar_t* VirtId(void) const override
        {
            return L"B3";
        }

        const wchar_t* Conflict(void) const { return L"B3::Conflict()"; }

};


class VirtualClass : virtual public B1,   virtual public B2
{
public:
        VirtualClass(void) :
            B1(),
            B2(),
            m_id(L"VirtualClass")
        { }

        virtual ~VirtualClass(void) { }

        const wchar_t* Id(void) const { return m_id.c_str(); }

        virtual const wchar_t* VirtId(void) const override
        {
            return m_id.c_str();
        }

private:
        wstring                     m_id;
};
```

```cpp
// Note: If you were trying to inherit from A before inheriting from B1
// and B3, there would be a Visual C++ compiler error. If you
// tried to inherit from it after B1 and B3, there would still be a
// compiler warning. If you both indirectly and directly inherit
// from a class, it is impossible to get at the direct inheritance
// version of it.
class NonVirtualClass : public B1, public B3
{
public:
    NonVirtualClass(void) :
        B1(),
        B3(),
        m_id(L"NonVirtualClass")
    { }

    virtual ~NonVirtualClass(void) { }

    const wchar_t* Id(void) const { return m_id.c_str(); }

    virtual const wchar_t* VirtId(void) const override
    {
        return m_id.c_str();
    }

    //// If we decided we wanted to use B1::Conflict, we could use
    //// a using declaration. In this case, we would be saying that
    //// calling NonVirtualClass::Conflict means call B1::Conflict
    //using B1::Conflict;

    //// We can also use it to resolve ambiguity between member
    //// data. In this case, we would be saying that
    //// NonVirtualClass::SomeInt means B3::SomeInt, so
    //// the nvC.SomeInt statement in
    //// DemonstrateNonVirtualInheritance would be legal, even
```

```cpp
        //// though IntelliSense says otherwise.
        //using B3::SomeInt;


private:
        wstring                         m_id;
};


void DemonstrateNonVirtualInheritance(void)
{
        NonVirtualClass nvC = NonVirtualClass();

        //// SomeInt is ambiguous since there are two copies of A, one
        //// indirectly from B1 and the other indirectly from B3.
        //nvC.SomeInt = 20;

        // But you can access the two copies of SomeInt by specifying which
        // base class' SomeInt you want. Note that if NonVirtualClass also
        // directly inherited from A, then this too would be impossible.
        nvC.B1::SomeInt = 20;
        nvC.B3::SomeInt = 20;

        //// It is impossible to create a reference to A due to ambiguity.
        //A& nvCA = nvC;

        // We can create references to B1 and B3 though.
        B1& nvCB1 = nvC;
        B3& nvCB3 = nvC;

        // If we want a reference to some particular A, we can now get one.
        A& nvCAfromB1 = nvCB1;
        A& nvCAfromB3 = nvCB3;

        // To demonstrate that there are two copies of A's data.
        wcout <<
                L"B1::SomeInt = " << nvCB1.SomeInt << endl <<
```

```
                L"B3::SomeInt = " << nvCB3.SomeInt << endl <<

        endl;


++nvCB1.SomeInt;
nvCB3.SomeInt += 20;


wcout <<
        L"B1::SomeInt = " << nvCB1.SomeInt << endl <<
        L"B3::SomeInt = " << nvCB3.SomeInt << endl <<
        endl;


// Let's see a final demo of the result. Note that the Conflict
// member function is also ambiguous because both B1 and B3 have
// a member function named Conflict with the same signature.
wcout <<
        typeid(nvC).name() << endl <<
        nvC.Id() << endl <<
        nvC.VirtId() << endl <<
        //// This is ambiguous between B1 and B3
        //nvC.Conflict() << endl <<
        // But we can solve that ambiguity.
        nvC.B3::Conflict() << endl <<
        nvC.B1::Conflict() << endl <<
        //// GetSomeInt is ambiguous too.
        //nvC.GetSomeInt() << endl <<
        endl <<


        typeid(nvCB3).name() << endl <<
        nvCB3.Id() << endl <<
        nvCB3.VirtId() << endl <<
        nvCB3.Conflict() << endl <<
        endl <<


        typeid(nvCB1).name() << endl <<
        nvCB1.Id() << endl <<
```

```cpp
            nvCB1.VirtId() << endl <<
            nvCB1.GetSomeInt() << endl <<
            nvCB1.Conflict() << endl <<
            endl;
}


void DemonstrateVirtualInheritance(void)
{
    VirtualClass vC = VirtualClass();

    // This works since VirtualClass has virtual inheritance of B1,
    // which has virtual inheritance of A, and VirtualClass has virtual
    // inheritance of A, which means all inheritances of A are virtual
    // and thus there is only one copy of A.
    vC.SomeInt = 20;

    // We can create a reference directly to A and also to B1 and B2.
    A& vCA = vC;
    B1& vCB1 = vC;
    B2& vCB2 = vC;

    // To demonstrate that there is just one copy of A's data.
    wcout <<
        L"B1::SomeInt = " << vCB1.SomeInt << endl <<
        L"B3::SomeInt = " << vCB2.SomeInt << endl <<
        endl;

    ++vCB1.SomeInt;
    vCB2.SomeInt += 20;

    wcout <<
        L"B1::SomeInt = " << vCB1.SomeInt << endl <<
        L"B3::SomeInt = " << vCB2.SomeInt << endl <<
        endl;
```

```cpp
// Let's see a final demo of the result. Note that the Conflict
// member function is still ambiguous because both B1 and B2 have
// a member function named Conflict with the same signature.
wcout <<
        typeid(vC).name() << endl <<
        vC.Id() << endl <<
        vC.VirtId() << endl <<
        vC.B2::Id() << endl <<
        vC.B2::VirtId() << endl <<
        vC.B1::Id() << endl <<
        vC.B1::VirtId() << endl <<
        vC.A::Id() << endl <<
        vC.A::VirtId() << endl <<
        // This is ambiguous between B1 and B2
        //vC.Conflict() << endl <<
        // But we can solve that ambiguity.
        vC.B2::Conflict() << endl <<
        vC.B1::Conflict() << endl <<
        // There's no ambiguity here because of virtual inheritance.
        vC.GetSomeInt() << endl <<
        endl <<


        typeid(vCB2).name() << endl <<
        vCB2.Id() << endl <<
        vCB2.VirtId() << endl <<
        vCB2.Conflict() << endl <<
        endl <<


        typeid(vCB1).name() << endl <<
        vCB1.Id() << endl <<
        vCB1.VirtId() << endl <<
        vCB1.GetSomeInt() << endl <<
        vCB1.Conflict() << endl <<
        endl <<
```

```
            typeid(vCA).name() << endl <<

            vCA.Id() << endl <<

            vCA.VirtId() << endl <<

            vCA.GetSomeInt() << endl <<

            endl;
}


int _pmain(int /*argc*/, _pchar* /*argv*/[])
{

        DemonstrateNonVirtualInheritance();

        DemonstrateVirtualInheritance();

        return 0;

}
```

 Note: Many of the member functions in the previous sample are declared as const by including the const *keyword after the parameter list in the declaration. This notation is part of the concept of const-correctness, which we will discuss elsewhere. The only thing that the const-member-function notation means is that the member function is not changing any member data of the class; you do not need to worry about side effects when calling it in a multi-threading scenario. The compiler enforces this notation so you can be sure a function you mark as const really is const.*

The previous sample demonstrates the difference between virtual member functions and non-virtual member functions. The Id function in class A is non-virtual while the VirtId function is virtual. The result is that when creating a base class reference to NonVirtualClass and call Id, we receive the base class' version of Id, whereas when we call VirtId, we receive NonVirtualClass's version of VirtId.

The same is true for VirtualClass, of course. Though the sample is careful to always specify virtual and override for the overrides of VirtId (and you should be too), as long as A::VirtId is declared as being virtual, then all derived class methods with the same signature will be considered virtual overrides of VirtId.

The previous sample also demonstrates the diamond problem that multiple-inheritance can produce as well as how virtual inheritance solves it. The *diamond problem* moniker comes from the idea that if class Z derives from class X and class Y, which both derive from class W, a diagram of this inheritance relationship would look like a diamond. Without virtual inheritance, the inheritance relationship does not actually form a diamond; instead, it forms a two-pronged fork with each prong having its own W.

NonVirtualClass has non-virtual inheritance from B1, which has virtual inheritance from A, and from B3, which has non-virtual inheritance from A. This results in a diamond problem, with two copies of the A class' member data becoming a part of

`NonVirtualClass`' member data. The `DemonstrateNonVirtualInheritance` function shows the problems that result from this and also shows the syntax used to resolve which A you want when you need to use one of A's members.

`VirtualClass` has virtual inheritance from both B1, which has virtual inheritance from A, and from B2, which also has virtual inheritance from A. Since all the inheritance chains that go from `VirtualClass` to A are virtual, there is only one copy of A's data; thus, the diamond problem is avoided. The `DemonstrateVirtualInheritance` function shows this.

Even with virtual inheritance, `VirtualClass` still has one ambiguity. `B1::Conflict` and `B2::Conflict` both have the same name and same parameters (none, in this case), so it is impossible to resolve which one you want without using the base-class-specifier syntax.

Naming is very important when dealing with multiple-inheritance if you wish to avoid ambiguity. There is, however, a way to resolve ambiguity. The two commented-out `using` declarations in `NonVirtualClass` demonstrate this resolution mechanism. If we decided we wanted to always resolve an ambiguity in a certain way, the `using` declaration lets us do that.

> *Note: The `using` declaration is useful for resolving ambiguity outside of a class too (within a namespace or a function, for instance). It is also useful if you wish to bring only certain types from a namespace into scope without bringing the entire namespace into scope with a `using namespace` directive. It is okay to use a `using` declaration within a header, provided it is inside a class, structure, union, or function definition, since `using` declarations are limited to the scope in which they exist. You should not use them outside of these since you would be bringing that type into scope within the global namespace or within whatever namespace you were in.*

One thing I did not touch on in the sample is inheritance access specifiers other than public. If you wanted, you could write something like `class B : protected class A { ... }`. Then class A's members would be accessible from within B's methods, and accessible to any class derived from B, but not *publicly* accessible. You could also say `class B : private class A { ... }`. Then class A's members would be accessible from within B's methods, but not accessible to any classes derived from B, nor would they be publicly accessible.

I mention these in passing simply because they are rarely used. You might, nonetheless, come across them, and you may even find a use for them. If so, remember that a class that privately inherits from a base class still has full access to that base class; you are simply saying that no further-derived classes should have access to the base class' member functions and variables.

More common, you will come across mistakes where you or someone else forgot to type `public` before a base class specifier, resulting in the default private inheritance. You'll recognize this by the slew of error messages telling you that you can't access private member functions or data of some base class, unless you are writing a library and don't test the class. In that case, you will recognize the issue from the angry roars of your users. One more reason unit testing is a good idea.

Abstract Classes

An abstract class has at least one pure virtual member function. The following sample shows how to mimic a C# interface.

Sample: AbstractClassSample\IWriteData.h

```cpp
#pragma once


class IWriteData
{
public:

    IWriteData(void) { }
    virtual ~IWriteData(void) { }


    virtual void Write(const wchar_t* value) = 0;
    virtual void Write(double value) = 0;
    virtual void Write(int value) = 0;


    virtual void WriteLine(void) = 0;
    virtual void WriteLine(const wchar_t* value) = 0;
    virtual void WriteLine(double value) = 0;
    virtual void WriteLine(int value) = 0;
};
```

Sample: AbstractClassSample\ConsoleWriteData.h

```cpp
#pragma once


#include "IWriteData.h"


class ConsoleWriteData :
    public IWriteData
{
public:

    ConsoleWriteData(void) { }
    virtual ~ConsoleWriteData(void) { }
```

```
        virtual void Write(const wchar_t* value);

        virtual void Write(double value);

        virtual void Write(int value);


        virtual void WriteLine(void);

        virtual void WriteLine(const wchar_t* value);

        virtual void WriteLine(double value);

        virtual void WriteLine(int value);

};
```

Sample: AbstractClassSample\ConsoleWriteData.cpp

```cpp
#include <iostream>

#include <ostream>

#include "ConsoleWriteData.h"


using namespace std;


void ConsoleWriteData::Write(const wchar_t* value)

{

        wcout << value;

}


void ConsoleWriteData::Write(double value)

{

        wcout << value;

}


void ConsoleWriteData::Write(int value)

{

        wcout << value;

}


void ConsoleWriteData::WriteLine(void)

{

        wcout << endl;

}
```

```cpp
void ConsoleWriteData::WriteLine(const wchar_t* value)
{

      wcout << value << endl;

}


void ConsoleWriteData::WriteLine(double value)
{

      wcout << value << endl;

}


void ConsoleWriteData::WriteLine(int value)
{

      wcout << value << endl;

}
```

Sample: AbstractClassSample\AbstractClassSample.cpp

```cpp
#include "IWriteData.h"

#include "ConsoleWriteData.h"

#include "../pchar.h"


int _pmain(int /*argc*/, _pchar* /*argv*/[])
{

      //// The following line is illegal since IWriteData is abstract.

      //IWriteData iwd = IWriteData();


      //// The following line is also illegal. You cannot have an

      //// instance of IWriteData.

      //IWriteData iwd = ConsoleWriteData();


      ConsoleWriteData cwd = ConsoleWriteData();


      // You can create an IWriteData reference to an instance of a class

      // that derives from IWriteData.

      IWriteData& r_iwd = cwd;
```

```
// You can also create an IWriteData pointer to an instance of a

// class that derives from IWriteData.

IWriteData* p_iwd = &cwd;


cwd.WriteLine(10);

r_iwd.WriteLine(14.6);

p_iwd->WriteLine(L"Hello Abstract World!");


return 0;

}
```

The previous sample demonstrates how to implement an interface-style class in C++. The IWriteData class could be inherited by a class that writes data to a log file, to a network connection, or to any other output. By passing around a pointer or a reference to IWriteData, you could easily switch output mechanisms.

The syntax for an abstract member function, called a pure virtual function, is simply to add = 0 after the declaration, as in IWriteData class: void Write(int value) = 0;. You do not need to make a class purely abstract; you can implement member functions or include member data common to all instances of the class. If a class has even one pure virtual function, then it is considered an abstract class.

Visual C++ provides a Microsoft-specific way to define an interface. Here's the equivalent of IWriteData using the Microsoft syntax:

Sample: AbstractClassSample\IWriteData.h

```
#pragma once


__interface IWriteData

{

    virtual void Write(const wchar_t* value) = 0;

    virtual void Write(double value) = 0;

    virtual void Write(int value) = 0;


    virtual void WriteLine(void) = 0;

    virtual void WriteLine(const wchar_t* value) = 0;

    virtual void WriteLine(double value) = 0;

    virtual void WriteLine(int value) = 0;

};
```

Rather than define it as a class, you define it using the `_interface` keyword. You cannot define a constructor, a destructor, or any member functions other than pure virtual member functions. You also cannot inherit from anything other than other interfaces. You do not need to include the `public` access specifier since all member functions are public.

Precompiled Header Files

A precompiled header file is a special type of header file. Like a normal header file, you can stick both include statements and code definitions in it. What it does differently is help to speed up compile times.

The precompiled header will be compiled the first time you build your program. From then on, as long as you don't make changes to the precompiled header, or to anything included directly or indirectly in the precompiled header, the compiler can reuse the existing compiled version of the precompiled header. Your compile times will speed up because a lot of code (e.g., Windows.h and the C++ Standard Library headers) will not be recompiled for each build.

If you use a precompiled header file, you need to include it as the first include statement of every source code file. You should not, however, include it in any header files. If you forget to include it, or put other include statements above it, then the compiler will generate an error. This requirement is a consequence of how precompiled headers work.

Precompiled header files are not part of the C++ standard. Their implementation depends on the compiler vendor. If you have any questions about them, you should look at the compiler vendor's documentation and make sure to specify which compiler you are using if you ask in an online forum.

Forward Declarations

As we've discussed, when you include a header file, the preprocessor simply takes all the code and inserts it right into the source code file that it is currently compiling. If that header file includes other header files, then all of those come in too.

Some header files are huge. Some include many other header files. Some are huge and include many other header files. The result is that a lot of code can wind up being compiled again and again simply because you include a header file in another header file.

One way to avoid the need to include header files within other header files is to use forward declarations. Consider the following code:

```
#pragma once


#include "SomeClassA.h"

#include "Flavor.h"

#include "Toppings.h"


class SomeClassB

{

public:

    SomeClassB(void);

    ~SomeClassB(void);


    int GetValueFromSomeClassA(

        const SomeClassA* value

        );


    bool CompareTwoSomeClassAs(

        const SomeClassA& first,

        const SomeClassA& second

        );


    void ChooseFlavor(

        Flavor flavor

        );
```

```
    void AddTopping(

        Toppings topping

        );


    void RemoveTopping(

        Toppings topping

        );


private:

    Toppings        m_toppings;

    Flavor          m_flavor;


    // Other member data and member functions...

};
```

We've included the **SomeClassA.h**, **Flavor.h**, and **Toppings.h** header files. SomeClassA is a class. Flavor is a scoped enum (specifically an enum class). Toppings is an un-scoped enum.

Look at our function definitions: We have a pointer to SomeClassA in GetValueFromSomeClassA. We have two references to SomeClassA in CompareTwoSomeClassAs. Then we have various uses of Flavor and Toppings.

In this case, we can eliminate all three of those include statements. Why? Because to compile this class definition, the compiler just needs to know the type of SomeClassA and the underlying data types of Flavor and Toppings. We can tell the compiler all of this with forward declarations.

```
#pragma once


class SomeClassA;

enum class Flavor;

enum Toppings : int;


class SomeClassB

{

public:

        SomeClassB(void);
```

```cpp
    ~SomeClassB(void);

    int GetValueFromSomeClassA(
        const SomeClassA* value
        );

    bool CompareTwoSomeClassAs(
        const SomeClassA& first,
        const SomeClassA& second
        );

    void ChooseFlavor(
        Flavor flavor
        );

    void AddTopping(
        Toppings topping
        );

    void RemoveTopping(
        Toppings topping
        );

private:
    Toppings        m_toppings;
    Flavor          m_flavor;

    // Other member data and member functions...
};
```

The three lines after #pragma once tell the compiler everything it needs to know. It's told that SomeClassA is a class, so it can establish its type for linkage purposes. It's told that Flavor is an enum class, and thus it knows that it needs to reserve space for an int (the default underlying type of an enum class). Lastly, it's told that Toppings is an enum with an underlying type of int, and thus it can reserve space for it as well.

If the definitions of those types in **SomeClassA.h**, **Flavor.h**, and **Toppings.h** did not match those forward declarations, then you would receive compiler errors. If you wanted a someClassA instance to be a member variable of someClassB, or if you wanted to pass one as an argument directly rather than as a pointer or a reference, then you would need to include someClassA. The compiler would then need to reserve space for someClassA and would need its full definition in order to determine its size in memory. Lastly, you still need to include those three header files in the **SomeClassB.cpp** source code file since you will be working with them within the someClassB member function definitions.

So what have we gained? Anytime you include **SomeClassB.h** in a source code file, that code file will not automatically contain all the code from **SomeClassA.h**, **Flavor.h**, and **Toppings.h** and compile with it. You might choose to include them if you need them, but you've eliminated their automatic inclusion and that of any header files they include.

Let's say **SomeClassA.h** includes **Windows.h** because, in addition to giving you some value, it also works with a window in your application. You've suddenly reduced the lines of code (by thousands and thousands) that need to be compiled in any source code file that includes **SomeClassB.h** but does not include **SomeClassA.h** or **Windows.h**. If you include **SomeClassB.h** in several dozen files, you're suddenly talking about tens to hundreds of thousands of lines of code.

Forward declarations can save a few milliseconds, or minutes, or hours (for large projects). They are not a magic solution to all problems of course, but they are a valuable tool that can save time when used properly.

Chapter 4   Storage Duration

Overview

To quote the C++ Language Standard, "Storage duration is the property of an object that defines the minimum potential lifetime of the storage containing the object." Basically, it's what tells you how long you should expect a variable to be usable. The variable might be a fundamental type, such as an `int`, or a complex type, such as a `class`. Regardless of its type, a variable is only guaranteed to last for as long as the programming language says it should.

C++ manages memory very differently from C#. For one thing, there is no requirement to have a garbage collector, and few implementations provide one. To the extent that C++ implementations do have automatic memory management, they mostly do so through smart pointers and reference counting. C++ classes do not automatically live on a heap (GC-managed or otherwise). Instead, they work much more like structures in C#.

You can push a C++ class instance onto a heap when you need to, but if you declare it locally and don't do anything funny, then it will have an automatic duration, typically implemented using a stack, and will be automatically destroyed when the program leaves the scope in which the class exists.

C++ gives you more control over memory management than C#. A consequence of this is that the C++ language and runtime environment cannot do as much to prevent erroneous code as the C# language and the CLR can. One of the keys to being a good C++ programmer is to understand how memory management works and to use the best practices in order to write efficient, correct code.

Static Duration

Global variables, including those inside namespaces, and variables marked with the duration keyword `static` have static storage duration.

Global variables are initialized during program initialization (i.e. the period before the program actually starts execution of your `main` or `wmain` function). They are initialized in the order in which they are defined in the source code. It's generally not a good idea to rely on initialization order since refactoring and other seemingly innocent changes could easily introduce a potential bug into your program.

Local statics are zero-initialized the first time program execution reaches the block containing the local static. Typically, they will be initialized to their specified values or initialized by calling the specified constructor at that point. The value assignment or construction phase is not required until the program reaches and executes the statement, except in very rare circumstances. Once a local static is initialized, the initialization specified with its declaration will never run again. This, of course, is just what we would expect of a local static. If it kept initializing itself every time the program reached its definition line, then it would be the same as a non-static local.

You can assign other values to global and local statics, unless you also make them `const`, of course.

Automatic Duration

Within a block, an object has automatic duration if it is defined without the `new` operator to instantiate it, and without a storage duration keyword, although it can optionally have the `register` keyword. This means the object is created at the point when it is defined and is destroyed when the program exits the block its variable was declared in, or when a new value is assigned to its variable.

Note: The auto keyword used to be a way of explicitly selecting automatic storage duration. In C++11, that usage was removed. It now is the equivalent of the var keyword in C#. If you try to compile something using the old meaning of auto, you'll receive a compiler error since auto as a type specifier must be the only type specifier.

Dynamic Duration

Dynamic duration is the result of using either the `new` operator or the `new[]` operator. The `new` operator is used to allocate single objects, while the `new[]` operator is used to allocate dynamic arrays. You must keep track of the size of a dynamically allocated array. While the C++ implementation will properly free a dynamically allocated array, provided you use the `delete[]` operator, there is no easy or portable way to determine the size of that allocation. It will likely be impossible. Single objects are freed with the `delete` operator.

When you allocate memory using `new` or `new[]`, the return value is a pointer. A pointer is a variable that holds a memory address. In C#, if you set all your references to an object to null or some other value, then the memory is no longer reachable in your program, so the GC can free that memory for other uses.

In C++, if you set all of your pointers to an object to `nullptr` or some other value, and you cannot figure out the original address using pointer arithmetic, then you have lost your ability to release that memory using the `delete` or `delete[]` operators. You have thereby created a memory leak. If a program leaks enough memory, eventually it will crash because the system will run out of memory addresses for it. Even before that, though, the computer will slow horribly, as it is forced to increase paging to accommodate the ever-increasing memory footprint of your program (assuming it has virtual memory, which is absent from most smart phones).

 Note: A const pointer, such as `someStr` *in the statement* `const wchar_t* someStr = L"Hello World!";` *is not a dynamic duration pointer. That memory is just part of the program itself. If you try to call* `delete` *or* `delete[]` *on it, the program will simply crash. A string is an array of characters, however, so if it were okay to delete it, then the* `delete[]` *operator would be the correct one to use.*

When dealing with dynamic memory, to eliminate potential leaks and limit the possibility of other related bugs, you should always use a smart pointer such as `std::unique_ptr` or `std::shared_ptr`. We will discuss these in the <u>chapter that covers pointers</u>.

Thread Duration

Thread duration is the least commonly used storage duration. It has only recently been standardized. As of this writing, few, if any, C++ compiler vendors have implemented support for the new `thread_local` keyword from the C++11 standard.

This is certain to change, but for now you can use vendor-specific extensions such as the Microsoft-specific extension `_declspec(thread)` or the GCC-specific extension `_thread` if you need functionality of this sort.

Thread duration is similar to static duration except instead of lasting the life of the program, these variables are local to each thread; the thread's copy exists for the duration of the thread. Each thread's instance of a thread duration object is initialized when it is first used in the thread, and it is destroyed when the thread exits. A thread duration object does not inherit its value from the thread that started the thread it exists in.

Choosing the Right Storage Duration

Automatic storage duration is usually the right form of storage duration for objects, unless you need them to survive the scope they were created in. If that is the case, you should pick one of the remaining storage durations that best fits your needs.

- If the object should exist for the whole length of the program's execution, use static storage duration.
- If the object should exist for the whole length of a particular thread, use thread storage duration.
- If the object will only exist for part of the program or thread's duration, use dynamic storage duration.

You can deviate from those recommendations if doing so makes sense, but in most cases, this guidance will steer you correctly.

Storage Duration Sample

The following sample is included to help clarify these concepts. The sample is heavily documented, so no additional commentary is included. I strongly encourage you to build and run this particular sample. Seeing the output while stepping through the code will help you grasp these concepts more easily than simply reading the code.

Sample: StorageDurationSample\SomeClass.h

```cpp
#pragma once

#include <string>

#include <memory>


class SomeClass
{
public:

    explicit SomeClass(int value = 0);

    SomeClass(
        int value,
        const wchar_t* stringId
        );


    ~SomeClass(void);

    int GetValue(void) { return m_value; }

    void SetValue(int value) { m_value = value; }

    static std::unique_ptr<SomeClass> s_someClass;

private:

    int                 m_value;

    std::wstring        m_stringId;
};
```

Sample: StorageDurationSample\SomeClass.cpp

```cpp
#include "SomeClass.h"

#include <string>

#include <ostream>

#include <iostream>

#include <ios>

#include <iomanip>

#include <thread>

#include <memory>


using namespace std;


SomeClass::SomeClass(int value) :

    m_value(value),

    m_stringId(L"(No string id provided.)")

{

    SomeClass* localThis = this;

    auto addr = reinterpret_cast<unsigned int>(localThis);

    wcout << L"Creating SomeClass instance." << endl <<

        L"StringId: " << m_stringId.c_str() << L"." << endl <<

        L"Address is: '0x" << setw(8) << setfill(L'0') <<

        hex << addr << dec << L"'." << endl <<

        L"Value is '" << m_value << L"'." << endl <<

        L"Thread id: '" <<

        this_thread::get_id() << L"'." << endl << endl;

}


SomeClass::SomeClass(

    int value,

    const wchar_t* stringId

    ) : m_value(value),

    m_stringId(stringId)

{

    SomeClass* localThis = this;

    auto addr = reinterpret_cast<int>(localThis);

    wcout << L"Creating SomeClass instance." << endl <<
```

```cpp
            L"StringId: " << m_stringId.c_str() << L"." << endl <<
            L"Address is: '0x" << setw(8) << setfill(L'0') <<
            hex << addr << dec << L"'." << endl <<
            L"Value is '" << m_value << L"'." << endl <<
            L"Thread id: '" <<
            this_thread::get_id() << L"'." << endl << endl;
}


SomeClass::~SomeClass(void)
{
    // This is just here to clarify that we aren't deleting a
    // new object when we replace an old object with it, despite
    // the order in which the Creating and Destroying output is
    // shown.
    m_value = 0;
    SomeClass* localThis = this;
    auto addr = reinterpret_cast<unsigned int>(localThis);
    wcout << L"Destroying SomeClass instance." << endl <<
        L"StringId: " << m_stringId.c_str() << L"." << endl <<
        L"Address is: '0x" << setw(8) << setfill(L'0') <<
        hex << addr << dec << L"'." << endl <<
        L"Thread id: '" <<
        this_thread::get_id() << L"'." << endl << endl;
}


// Note that when creating a static member variable, the definition also
// needs to have the type specified. Here, we start off with
// 'unique_ptr<SomeClass>' before proceeding to the
// 'SomeClass::s_someClass = ...;' value assignment.
unique_ptr<SomeClass> SomeClass::s_someClass =
    unique_ptr<SomeClass>(new SomeClass(10, L"s_someClass"));
```

Sample: StorageDurationSample\StorageDurationSample.cpp

```cpp
#include <iostream>
#include <ostream>
#include <sstream>
```

```cpp
#include <thread>
#include <memory>
#include <cstddef>
#include "SomeClass.h"
#include "../pchar.h"

using namespace std;

struct SomeStruct
{
    int Value;
};

namespace Value
{
    // Visual C++ does not support thread_local as of VS 2012 RC. We can
    // partially mimic thread_local with _declspec(thread), but we cannot
    // have things as classes with functions (including constructors
    // and destructors) with _declspec(thread).
    _declspec(thread) SomeStruct ThreadLocalSomeStruct = {};


    // g_staticSomeClass has static duration. It exists until the program
    // ends or until a different value is assigned to it. Even if you left
    // off the static keyword, in this case it would still be static since
    // it is not a local variable, is not dynamic, and is not a thread-
    // local variable.
    static SomeClass g_staticSomeClass = SomeClass(20, L"g_staticSomeClass");

}


// This method creates a SomeClass instance, and then changes the
// value.
void ChangeAndPrintValue(int value)
{
    // Create an identifier string.
    wstringstream wsStr(L"");
```

```
        wsStr << L"ChangeAndPrintValue thread id: '" << this_thread::get_id()
            << L"'";
        // Create a SomeClass instance to demonstrate function-level block scope.
        SomeClass sc(value, wsStr.str().c_str());

        // Demonstrate _declspec(thread).
        wcout << L"Old value is " << Value::ThreadLocalSomeStruct.Value <<
            L". Thread id: '" << this_thread::get_id() << L"'." << endl;
        Value::ThreadLocalSomeStruct.Value = value;
        wcout << L"New value is " << Value::ThreadLocalSomeStruct.Value <<
            L". Thread id: '" << this_thread::get_id() << L"'." << endl;
}


void LocalStatic(int value)
{
        static SomeClass sc(value, L"LocalStatic sc");

        //// If you wanted to reinitialize sc every time, you would have to
        //// un-comment the following line. This, however, would defeat the
        //// purpose of having a local static. You could do something
        //// similar if you wanted to reinitialize it in certain circumstances
        //// since that would justify having a local static.
        //sc = SomeClass(value, L"LocalStatic_reinitialize");

        wcout << L"Local Static sc value: '" << sc.GetValue() <<
            L"'." << endl << endl;
}


int _pmain(int /*argc*/, _pchar* /*argv*/[])
{
        // Automatic storage; destroyed when this function ends.
        SomeClass sc1(1, L"_pmain sc1");
        wcout << L"sc1 value: '" << sc1.GetValue() <<
            L"'." << endl << endl;
        {
```

```
        // The braces here create a new block. This means that
        // sc2 only survives until the matching closing brace, since
        // it also has automatic storage.
        SomeClass sc2(2, L"_pmain sc2");
        wcout << L"sc2 value: '" << sc2.GetValue() <<
            L"'." << endl << endl;
    }


    LocalStatic(1000);
    // Note: The local static in LocalStatic will not be reinitialized
    // with 5000. See the function definition for more info.
    LocalStatic(5000);


    // To demonstrate _declspec(thread) we change the value of this
    // thread's Value::ThreadLocalSomeStruct to 20 from its default 0.
    ChangeAndPrintValue(20);


    // We now create a new thread that automatically starts and
    // changes the value of Value::ThreadLocalSomeStruct to 40. If it
    // were shared between threads, then it would be 20 from the
    // previous call to ChangeAndPrintValue. But it's not. Instead, it
    // is the default 0 that we would expect as a result of this being
    // a new thread.
    auto thr = thread(ChangeAndPrintValue, 40);


    // Wait for the thread we just created to finish executing. Note that
    // calling join from a UI thread is a bad idea since it blocks
    // the current thread from running until the thread we are calling
    // join on completes. For WinRT programming, you want to make use
    // of the PPLTasks API instead.
    thr.join();


    // Dynamic storage. WARNING: This is a 'naked' pointer, which is a very
    // bad practice. It is here to clarify dynamic storage and to serve
    // as an example. Normally, you should use either
```

```cpp
    // std::unique_ptr or std::shared_ptr to wrap any memory allocated with
    // the 'new' keyword or the 'new[]' keyword.
    SomeClass* p_dsc = new SomeClass(1000, L"_pmain p_dsc");


    const std::size_t arrIntSize = 5;


    // Dynamic storage array. THE SAME WARNING APPLIES.
    int* p_arrInt = new int[arrIntSize];


    // Note that there's no way to find how many elements arrInt
    // has other than to manually track it. Also note that the values in
    // arrInt are not initialized (i.e. it's not arrIntSize zeroes, it's
    // arrIntSize arbitrary integer values).


    for (int i = 0; i < arrIntSize; i++)
    {
        wcout << L"i: '" << i << L"'. p_arrInt[i] = '" <<
            p_arrInt[i] << L"'." << endl;


        // Assign a value of i to this index.
        p_arrInt[i] = i;
    }


    wcout << endl;

    //// If you wanted to zero out your dynamic array, you could do this:
    //uninitialized_fill_n(p_arrInt, arrIntSize, 0);


    for (int i = 0; i < arrIntSize; i++)
    {
        wcout << L"i: '" << i << L"'. p_arrInt[i] = '" <<
            p_arrInt[i] << L"'." << endl;
    }


    // If you forgot this, you would have a memory leak.
```

```cpp
    delete p_dsc;

    //// If you un-commented this, then you would have a double delete,
    //// which would crash your program.
    //delete p_dsc;

    //// If you did this, you would have a program error, which may or may
    //// not crash your program. Since dsc is not an array, it should not
    //// use the array delete (i.e. delete[]), but should use the non-array
    //// delete shown previously.
    //delete[] p_dsc;

    // You should always set a pointer to nullptr after deleting it to
    // prevent any accidental use of it (since what it points to is unknown
    // at this point).
    p_dsc = nullptr;

    // If you forgot this, you would have a memory leak. If you used
    // 'delete' instead of 'delete[]' unknown bad things might happen. Some
    // implementations will overlook it while others would crash or do who
    // knows what else.
    delete[] p_arrInt;
    p_arrInt = nullptr;

    wcout << L"Ending program." << endl;
    return 0;
}
```

For whom it is inconvenient to run the sample, here is the output I get when I run this from a command prompt on Windows 8 Release Preview, compiled with Visual Studio 2012 Ultimate RC in Debug configuration targeting the x86 chipset. You will probably produce different values for the addresses and thread IDs if you run it on your own system.

```
Creating SomeClass instance.
StringId: s_someClass.
Address is: '0x009fade8'.
```

```
Value is '10'.
Thread id: '3660'.


Creating SomeClass instance.
StringId: g_staticSomeClass.
Address is: '0x013f8554'.
Value is '20'.
Thread id: '3660'.


Creating SomeClass instance.
StringId: _pmain sc1.
Address is: '0x007bfe98'.
Value is '1'.
Thread id: '3660'.


sc1 value: '1'.


Creating SomeClass instance.
StringId: _pmain sc2.
Address is: '0x007bfe70'.
Value is '2'.
Thread id: '3660'.


sc2 value: '2'.


Destroying SomeClass instance.
StringId: _pmain sc2.
Address is: '0x007bfe70'.
Thread id: '3660'.


Creating SomeClass instance.
StringId: LocalStatic sc.
Address is: '0x013f8578'.
Value is '1000'.
Thread id: '3660'.
```

Local Static sc value: '1000'.

Local Static sc value: '1000'.

Creating SomeClass instance.

StringId: ChangeAndPrintValue thread id: '3660'.

Address is: '0x007bfbf4'.

Value is '20'.

Thread id: '3660'.

Old value is 0. Thread id: '3660'.

New value is 20. Thread id: '3660'.

Destroying SomeClass instance.

StringId: ChangeAndPrintValue thread id: '3660'.

Address is: '0x007bfbf4'.

Thread id: '3660'.

Creating SomeClass instance.

StringId: ChangeAndPrintValue thread id: '5796'.

Address is: '0x0045faa8'.

Value is '40'.

Thread id: '5796'.

Old value is 0. Thread id: '5796'.

New value is 40. Thread id: '5796'.

Destroying SomeClass instance.

StringId: ChangeAndPrintValue thread id: '5796'.

Address is: '0x0045faa8'.

Thread id: '5796'.

Creating SomeClass instance.

StringId: _pmain p_dsc.

Address is: '0x009fbcc0'.

Value is '1000'.

Thread id: '3660'.

i: '0'. p_arrInt[i] = ' 042150451'.

i: '1'. p_arrInt[i] = '-842150451'.

i: '2'. p_arrInt[i] = '-842150451'.

i: '3'. p_arrInt[i] = '-842150451'.

i: '4'. p_arrInt[i] = '-842150451'.

i: '0'. p_arrInt[i] = '0'.

i: '1'. p_arrInt[i] = '1'.

i: '2'. p_arrInt[i] = '2'.

i: '3'. p_arrInt[i] = '3'.

i: '4'. p_arrInt[i] = '4'.

Destroying SomeClass instance.

StringId: _pmain p_dsc.

Address is: '0x009fbcc0'.

Thread id: '3660'.

Ending program.

Destroying SomeClass instance.

StringId: _pmain sc1.

Address is: '0x007bfe98'.

Thread id: '3660'.

Destroying SomeClass instance.

StringId: LocalStatic sc.

Address is: '0x013f8578'.

Thread id: '3660'.

Destroying SomeClass instance.

StringId: g_staticSomeClass.

Address is: '0x013f8554'.

Thread id: '3660'.

Destroying SomeClass instance.

```
StringId: s_someClass.

Address is: '0x009fade8'.

Thread id: '3660'.
```

Chapter 5   Constructors, Destructors, and Operators

Overview

C++ constructors are more complicated than their C# counterparts. For one thing, there are five types of constructors. Although you will rarely write all five types for any particular class or structure, you do need to know what they are, what they do, and what they look like. If not, you could find yourself facing some very confusing bugs or compiler errors.

The reason C++ constructors are more involved than C# constructors is the variety in storage duration that a C++ class can have. By default, C++ objects have value semantics while C# classes have reference semantics. Here's an example:

```
Vehicle someVehicle = vehicle;
```

Let's assume `vehicle` is not null but is a valid object of type `Vehicle`, and that the `Vehicle` type is a class type as opposed to a structure or something else.

Let's consider the previous code statement as if it were C# code. In C#, the object that `vehicle` refers to lives off somewhere in a heap managed by the GC. The previous code statement stores a reference to that object in the `someVehicle` variable, which it gets from the existing `vehicle` reference to the object. There is still just the one instance of that object with two references to it.

Let's now consider the previous code statement as if it were C++ code. In C++, the object that `vehicle` refers to is likely an automatic duration object, but it could be a static duration object or even a thread duration object. The previous code statement would by default create a copy of the `vehicle` object and store it in the address of the automatic duration `someVehicle` variable. It does this using something called a copy assignment operator, a close relative of a copy constructor.

There are now two copies where once there was one. Unless the Vehicle class has a pointer, a `std::shared_ptr`, a reference, or something of that sort as a member variable, the two copies are completely separate. Changing or even destroying one will have no effect whatsoever on the other.

Of course, if you want `someVehicle` to be a reference to `vehicle`'s object, you can change the code slightly and accomplish that. But what if you wanted `someVehicle` to become `vehicle` and for `vehicle` to stop existing—to be destroyed without taking its former resources with it? C++ makes this possible through something called a move constructor and a move assignment operator.

If you want to intentionally disable copy semantics (assignment and construction, collectively) or move semantics, that is possible too.

Default Constructor

We'll start with default constructors. A default constructor can be called with no arguments. A class can have no more than one default constructor. If you define a class and include no constructors, you produce an implicit default constructor, which the compiler creates for you. However, if you have a class member variable that is a class, structure, or union that has no default constructor, then you must define at least one constructor because the compiler cannot create an implicit default constructor.

If you define a constructor with no parameters, it is an explicit default constructor. It is also possible to define a constructor that takes parameters and still make it a default constructor using default arguments, which we will discuss in a moment.

If you define a constructor that has at least one required parameter, then the compiler will not generate a default constructor. You must define an explicit default constructor if you want one.

Default Arguments in Function Declarations

Constructors in C++, and functions in general, can have default arguments specified for some or all of their parameters as part of their declaration (similar to C#'s optional arguments). In C++ functions, all parameters with default arguments must occur to the right of any parameter without a default argument in the function declaration. C++ does not support C#-style named arguments, but you can accomplish something similar using the named parameter idiom.

Why mention default arguments here? Well, it turns out that if you have a constructor in which all the parameters have default arguments, that constructor is a default constructor. It makes sense, since if you have a constructor with the signature `Vehicle(VehicleType type = VehicleType::Car, double odometerReading = 0.0);` then you can call that constructor with empty parentheses, and those default arguments will be applied. If you define a default constructor, you can have only one, regardless whether it has no parameters, or whether its parameters all have default arguments.

This principle goes further still. No two functions with the same name that are declared in the same scope can have the same parameter types in exactly the same positions. You guessed it: Parameters with default arguments are disregarded for the purpose of distinct function signatures.

It all makes sense because default arguments make it impossible to distinguish between `double Add(double a, double b = 0.0);` and `double Add(double a, int a = 0);` given that both could be called as `double dbl = Add(5.0);`. The compiler cannot know which you intended in that case, so it simply fails to compile and displays an error message.

Parameterized Constructors

A parameterized constructor has one or more parameters. A parameterized constructor where all of the parameters have default arguments is also the default constructor for a class. There is nothing special about parameterized constructors in C++.

Conversion Constructors

A conversion constructor has at least one parameter. If there is more than one, then those additional parameters must have default arguments.

If you do not want a constructor to be a conversion constructor, you can mark it with the function specifier: explicit. Let's look at an example:

```cpp
#include <string>


class SomeClass
{
public:
    SomeClass(const wchar_t* value) :
        m_strValue(value),
        m_intValue()
    {
    }


    explicit SomeClass(int value) :
        m_strValue(),
        m_intValue(value)
    {
    }


    ~SomeClass(void) { }


    const wchar_t* GetStringValue(void)
    {
        return m_strValue.c_str();
    }


    int GetIntValue(void) { return m_intValue; }

private:
    std::wstring        m_strValue;

    int                 m_intValue;
```

```
};

void DoSomething(void)
{
    // Normal constructor use.
    SomeClass sc1 = SomeClass(L"Hello World");

    // Fine because the const wchar_t* constructor
    // is a conversion constructor.
    SomeClass sc2 = L"Hello World";

    // Normal constructor use.
    SomeClass sc3 = SomeClass(1);

    //// Illegal since the int constructor is not a
    //// conversion constructor.
    //SomeClass sc4 = 1;

    // ...
}
```

As you can see, the conversion constructor lets us construct s2 by directly setting it equal to a string value. The compiler sees that statement, checks to see if someClass has a conversion constructor that will receive that sort of value, and proceeds to call the appropriate someClass constructor. If we tried that with the commented-out sc4 line, the complier would fail because we used explicit to tell the compiler that the constructor, which just takes int, should not be treated as a conversion constructor, but instead should be like any other parameterized constructor.

Conversion constructors can be useful, but they can also lead to bugs. For example, you could accidentally create a new object and assign it to an existing variable when you merely mistyped a variable name and really meant an assignment. The compiler won't complain if there is a valid conversion constructor, but will complain if there isn't. So keep that in mind and remember to mark single parameter constructors as explicit, except when you have a good reason for providing a conversion constructor.

Initialization of Data and Base Classes

By this point, we have seen quite a few constructors, so it's important to discuss the strange syntax you've encountered. Let's examine a sample:

 Note: This sample uses some very bad code practices in order to illustrate how C++ performs initialization. Specifically, the ordering of initializers in constructor definitions is misleading in some places. Always make sure your constructors order their initialization of base classes and parameters in the order that the initialization will actually occur during program execution. That will help you avoid bugs and make your code easier to debug and easier to follow.

Sample: InitializationSample\InitializationSample.cpp

```cpp
#include <iostream>

#include <ostream>

#include "../pchar.h"


using namespace std;


int CallingMsg(const wchar_t* cls)

{

    wcout << L"Calling " << cls << L" constructor." << endl;

    return 0;

}


int InitializingIntMsg(int value, const wchar_t* mvarName)

{

    wcout << L"Initializing " << mvarName << L"." << endl;

    return value;

}


class A

{

public:

    A(void) :

        m_value(InitializingIntMsg(5, L"DEFAULT m_value"))

        {

            wcout << L"DEFAULT Constructing A. m_value is '" <<
```

```cpp
                    m_value << L"'." << endl;
        }

        explicit A(int) :
                m_value(InitializingIntMsg(20, L"m_value"))
        {
                wcout << L"Constructing A. m_value is '" <<
                        m_value << L"'." << endl;
        }

        virtual ~A(void)
        {
                wcout << L"Destroying A." << endl;
        }

private:
        int        m_value;
};

class B : virtual public A
{
public:
        explicit B(int) :
                A(CallingMsg(L"A")),
                m_b(InitializingIntMsg(2, L"m_b")),
                m_a(InitializingIntMsg(5, L"m_a"))
        {
                wcout << L"Constructing B. m_a is '" <<
                        m_a << L"' and m_b is '" << m_b << L"'." << endl;
        }
        virtual ~B(void)
        {
                wcout << L"Destroying B." << endl;
        }
```

```cpp
private:

    int         m_a;

    int         m_b;
};


class C
{
public:

    explicit C(int) :

        m_c(InitializingIntMsg(0, L"m_c"))

    {

        wcout << L"Constructing C. m_c is '" <<

            m_c << L"'." << endl;

    }

    virtual ~C(void)

    {

        wcout << L"Destroying C." << endl;

    }


private:

    int m_c;
};


class D
{
public:

    explicit D(int) :

        m_d(InitializingIntMsg(3, L"m_d"))

    {

        wcout << L"Constructing D. m_d is '" <<

            m_d << L"'." << endl;

    }

    virtual ~D(void)

    {

        wcout << L"Destroying D." << endl;
```

```cpp
    }

private:
    int         m_d;
};

class Y : virtual public B, public D, virtual public C
{
public:
    explicit Y(int value) :
        C(CallingMsg(L"C")),
        m_someInt(InitializingIntMsg(value, L"m_someInt")),
        D(CallingMsg(L"D")),
        B(CallingMsg(L"B"))
    {
        wcout << L"Constructing Y. m_someInt is '" <<
            m_someInt << L"'." << endl;
    }
    virtual ~Y(void)
    {
        wcout << L"Destroying Y." << endl;
    }


    int GetSomeInt(void) { return m_someInt; }

private:
    int   m_someInt;
};

class Z : public D, virtual public B, public C
{
public:
    explicit Z(int value) :
        D(CallingMsg(L"D")),
        A(CallingMsg(L"A")),
```

```cpp
            C(CallingMsg(L"C")),
            m_someInt(InitializingIntMsg(value, L"m_someInt")),
            B(CallingMsg(L"B"))
        {
            wcout << L"Constructing Z. m_someInt is '" <<
                m_someInt << L"'." << endl;
        }
        virtual ~Z(void)
        {
            wcout << L"Destroying Z." << endl;
        }


        int GetSomeInt(void) { return m_someInt; }

private:
        int    m_someInt;
};


int _pmain(int /*argc*/, _pchar* /*argv*/[])
{
        {
            Y someY(CallingMsg(L"Y"));
            wcout << L"Y::GetSomeInt returns '" <<
                someY.GetSomeInt() << L"'." << endl;
        }


        wcout << endl << "Break between Y and Z." << endl
            << endl;


        {
            Z someZ(CallingMsg(L"Z"));
            wcout << L"Z::GetSomeInt returns '" <<
                someZ.GetSomeInt() << L"'." << endl;
        }
        return 0;
```

}

The first thing we've done is define two helper functions that write messages, so we can easily follow the order in which things are happening. You will notice that each of the classes has a constructor that takes `int`, though only `Y` and `Z` put it to use. `A`, `B`, `C`, and `D` do not even specify a name for the `int` in their `int` parameter constructors; they just specify that there is an `int` parameter. This is perfectly legal C++ code, and we've been using it all along with our commented-out parameter names in `_pmain`.

Class `A` has two constructors: a default constructor and a parameterized constructor that takes an `int`. The remaining classes have only parameterized constructors, each of which takes an `int`.

- Class `B` inherits from `A` virtually.
- Class `C` inherits from nothing.
- Class `D` inherits from nothing.
- Class `Y` inherits from `B` virtually, from `D` directly, and from `C` virtually, in that order.
- Class `Z` also inherits from `D` directly, from `B` virtually, and from `C` directly, in that order.

Let's look at the output this program gives us and then discuss what is happening and why.

```
Calling Y constructor.

Initializing DEFAULT m_value.

DEFAULT Constructing A. m_value is '5'.

Calling B constructor.

Initializing m_a.

Initializing m_b.

Constructing B. m_a is '5' and m_b is '2'.

Calling C constructor.

Initializing m_c.

Constructing C. m_c is '0'.

Calling D constructor.

Initializing m_d.

Constructing D. m_d is '3'.

Initializing m_someInt.

Constructing Y. m_someInt is '0'.

Y::GetSomeInt returns '0'.

Destroying Y.
```

```
Destroying D.

Destroying C.

Destroying B.

Destroying A.


Break between Y and Z.


Calling Z constructor.

Calling A constructor.

Initializing m_value.

Constructing A. m_value is '20'.

Calling B constructor.

Initializing m_a.

Initializing m_b.

Constructing B. m_a is '5' and m_b is '2'.

Calling D constructor.

Initializing m_d.

Constructing D. m_d is '3'.

Calling C constructor.

Initializing m_c.

Constructing C. m_c is '0'.

Initializing m_someInt.

Constructing Z. m_someInt is '0'.

Z::GetSomeInt returns '0'.

Destroying Z.

Destroying C.

Destroying D.

Destroying B.

Destroying A.
```

In our _pmain function, first we create an object of type Y within its own scope. We then call its GetSomeInt member function. This helps ensure that the compiler will not optimize away the creation of Y in a release build in case you mess around with the code. It also serves as a marker between construction and destruction.

We then exit the scope of Y, triggering its destruction. After this, we write another marker string to separate the instantiation of a Y instance from the instantiation of the

Z instance that follows. We create the Z instance in its own scope so we can follow its construction and destruction the same way as with Y.

So what do we see? Quite a lot. Let's focus on Y first.

When we call the Y constructor, the first thing it does is call the default constructor for A. This might seem terribly wrong for several reasons, but it is, in fact, right. The Y constructor says to follow this order:

1. Initialize base class C.
2. Initialize Y's member variable `m_someInt`.
3. Initialize base class D.
4. Initialize base class B.

Instead, we wind up with this order:

1. Initialize base class A via its default constructor.
2. Initialize base class B.
3. Initialize base class C.
4. Initialize base class D.
5. Initialize Y's member variable `m_someInt`.

Since we know B inherits virtually from A, and that B is the only source of inheritance from A, we can conclude that B is given priority over the others and that A is given priority over B.

Well, we inherit from B before we inherit from the other classes. So that could be it, but why doesn't D become initialized right after B? It's because D is directly inherited while C is virtually inherited. The virtuals come first.

Here are the rules:

1. Virtual base classes are constructed in a left-to-right order as they are written in the list of base classes.
2. If you do not call a specific constructor for a base class you have virtually inherited from, the compiler will automatically call its default constructor at the appropriate time.
3. When determining the order of base classes to construct, base classes are initialized before their derived classes.
4. When virtual base classes have all been constructed, then direct base classes are constructed in their left-to-right declaration order—the same as virtual base classes.
5. When all of its base classes have been constructed, a member variable of a class is:

- o Default-initialized if there is no initializer for it.
- o Value-initialized if the initializer is an empty set of parentheses.
- o Initialized to the result of the expression within the initializer's parentheses.

6. Member variables are initialized in the order they are declared in the class definition.
7. When all the initializers in a constructor have run, any code inside the constructor's body will be executed.

> Default initialization gives no initialization for fundamental types and for pointers. It calls the default constructor for class types. Integers, pointers, and the like will just have arbitrary values.
>
> Value initialization initializes fundamental types to zero or the equivalent (e.g., `false` for `bool` and null for pointers). It calls the default constructor for class types.

When you put all of these rules together, you initially find the order B, C, D because B and C have virtual inheritance and thus come before D. Then we add A before B because B derives from A. So we end up with A, B, C, D.

Because of the rule that base classes are initialized before derived classes, and because A comes in through virtual inheritance, A is initialized with its default constructor before we even get to its initializer in the B constructor that we call. Once we do get to the B constructor, because A is already initialized, its initializer in the B constructor is simply ignored.

Class B's member variables are initialized in the order m_a, m_b because that is the order they are declared in the class, even though in the constructor we list their initializations in the opposite order.

Delegating Constructor

 Note: Visual C++ does not support delegating constructors in Visual Studio 2012 RC.

A delegating constructor calls another constructor of the same class (the target constructor). The delegating constructor can have only one initializer statement, which is the call to the target constructor. Its body can have statements; these will run after the target constructor has completely finished. Here's an example:

```cpp
#include <iostream>
#include <ostream>

using namespace std;

class SomeClass
{
public:
    SomeClass(void) : SomeClass(10)
    {
        // Statements here will execute after the
        // statements in the SomeClass(int) constructor
        // body have finished executing.
        wcout << "Running SomeClass::SomeClass(void)." << endl;
    }

    SomeClass(int value)
        : m_value(value)
    {
        // Statements here will execute after the m_value
        // initializer above.
        wcout << "Running SomeClass::SomeClass(int)." << endl;
    }

    int GetValue(void) { return m_value; }
```

```
private:

    int         m_value;

};


int main(int argc, char* argv[])

{

    SomeClass someC;
    wcout << L"SomeClass::GetValue() = " << someC.GetValue() << endl;


    return 0;

}
```

If you compile and run that code using a compiler such as GCC, you will see the following output:

```
Running SomeClass::SomeClass(int).

Running SomeClass::SomeClass(void).

SomeClass::GetValue() = 10
```

Copy Constructor

A copy constructor has only one mandatory parameter: a reference to a variable having the same type as the constructor's class. A copy constructor can have other parameters as long as they are all provided with default arguments. Its purpose is to allow you to construct a copy of an object.

The compiler will provide you with a default copy constructor if it can, and it can as long as all the member variables that are classes, structures, or unions have a copy constructor. The copy constructor it provides is a shallow copy constructor. If you have a pointer to an array of data, for instance, the copy gets a copy of the pointer, not a new array containing a copy of the same data.

If you then had a delete statement in the destructor for that class, you would have one copy in an invalid state when the other was destroyed, and you'd have a runtime error when you tried to delete the memory for the second time when the remaining copy was destroyed, assuming your program had not already crashed. This is one of many reasons you should always use smart pointers. We will cover them in the chapter on RAII.

If you do not wish to use the compiler-provided copy constructor, or if the compiler cannot provide one, but you want to have one anyway, you can write a copy constructor. For example, perhaps you want a deeper copy of the data, or perhaps your class has a `std::unique_ptr` and you decide what an acceptable "copy" of it would be for the purposes of your class. We will see an example of this in **ConstructorsSample**.

A copy constructor should typically have the following declaration: `SomeClass(const SomeClass&);`. To avoid weird errors, the constructor should always take a `const` lvalue reference to the class you copy from. There's no reason you should change the class you are copying from in a copy constructor. Making it `const` does no harm and provides some guarantees about your operation. A copy constructor should not be defined as `explicit`.

Copy Assignment Operator

If you define a custom copy constructor, you should also define a custom copy assignment operator. The result of this operator should be that the returned value is a copy of the class it is copying. This is what is invoked when you have a statement such as `a = b;` where `a` and `b` are both of the same type (e.g., `SomeClass`).

This operator is a non-static member function of its class, so it is only invoked when you are copy-assigning to an existing instance of the class. If you had something like `SomeClass a = b;` then it would be a copy construction, not a copy assignment.

A copy assignment operator should have the following declaration: `SomeClass& operator= (const SomeClass&);`.

Move Constructor

In C++, if all you had was a copy constructor, and you wanted to pass a class instance into a `std::vector` (similar to a .NET `List<T>`) or return it from a function, you would need to make a copy of it. Even if you had no intention of using it again, you would still incur the time it takes to make a copy. If you're adding many elements to a `std::vector`, or if you wrote a factory function that you use a lot, it would be a big performance hit.

This is why C++ has a move constructor. The move constructor is new in C++11. There are some circumstances in which the compiler will provide you one, but generally you should write your own for the classes you will need it for.

It's easy to do. Note that if you write a move constructor, then you will also need to write a copy constructor. Visual C++ does not enforce this rule as of Visual Studio 2012 RC, but it is part of the C++ language standard. If you need to compile your program with another compiler, you should make sure that you write copy constructors and copy assignment operators when you write a move constructor.

A move constructor should typically have the following declaration: `SomeClass(SomeClass&&);`. It cannot be `const` (because we will be modifying it) or `explicit`.

`std::move`

The `std::move` function helps you write move constructors and move assignment operators. It's in the `<utility>` header file. It takes a single argument and returns it in a condition suitable for moving. The object passed in will be returned as an `rvalue` reference, unless move semantics were disabled for it, in which case you will get a compiler error.

Move Assignment Operator

Whenever you write a move constructor for a class, you should also write a move assignment operator. The result of this operator should be that the returned value contains all the data of the old class. A proper move assignment operator can be called from your move constructor in order to avoid code duplication.

A move assignment operator should have the following declaration: `SomeClass& operator=(SomeClass&&);`.

Removing Copy or Move Semantics

If you need to remove copy or move semantics, there are two ways to do this. First, to remove copy semantics, you can declare the copy constructor and copy assignment operator as private and leave them unimplemented. C++ only cares about an implementation of a function if you attempt to use it. By doing this, any attempt to compile a program that is trying to use copy semantics will fail, producing error messages saying you are trying to use a private member of the class and there is no implementation for it (if you accidentally use it within the class itself). The same pattern of making the constructor and assignment operator private works equally well for move semantics.

The second way is new to C++11 and is currently unsupported by Visual C++ as of Visual Studio 2012 RC. With this way, you would declare the functionality as explicitly being deleted. For example, to explicitly delete a copy constructor, you would write `SomeClass(const SomeClass&) = delete;`. The same `= delete` syntax applies to assignment operators, the move constructor, and any other functionality. However, until Visual C++ supports it, you will need to stick with the first way.

Destructors and Virtual Destructors

Any class serving as the base class of another class should have a virtual destructor. You declare a virtual destructor using the `virtual` keyword, (e.g., : `virtual ~SomeClass(void) ;`). This way, if you cast an object down to one of its subclasses, and then subsequently destroy the object, the proper constructor will be called, ensuring that all of the resources the class had captured are freed.

Proper destructors are critical to the RAII idiom, which we will explore shortly. You should never allow an exception to be thrown in a destructor unless you catch and handle that exception within the destructor. If there is an exception you cannot handle, you should perform safe error logging and then exit from the program. You can use the `std::terminate` function in the `<exception>` header file to invoke the current terminate handler. By default, the terminate handler invokes the `abort` function from the `<cstdlib>` header. We will discuss this functionality further in our exploration of C++ Standard Library exceptions.

Operator Overloading

Operator overloading is a powerful, advanced feature of C++. You can overload operators on a per-class basis or globally with a stand-alone function. Almost every operator in C++ can be overloaded. We will see examples of overloading the copy assignment, move assignment, &, |, and |= operators shortly. For a list of other operators you can overload, and how such overloads work, I recommend visiting the MSDN documentation on the subject. It's a useful feature, but one you may not commonly use. Looking it up when you need it is often faster than trying to memorize it right away.

> *Tip: Don't overload an operator to give it a meaning that is likely to be confusing and contrary to someone's expectations of what that overload does. For example, the + operator should generally perform an addition or concatenation operation. Making it subtract, split, divide, multiply, or anything else that would seem odd will confuse others and introduce a strong potential for bugs. This does not mean you shouldn't put operators without clear semantic meaning in a particular situation to use. The std::wcout and std::wcin I/O functionality from the C++ Standard Library puts the >> and << operators to use in writing and reading data.*
>
> *Since bit shifting would not have a particular meaning when applied to streams, repurposing these operators in this way seems odd and different, but does not lend itself to any clearly wrong conclusions about their purpose. Once you understand what the operators do when applied to streams, repurposing them adds functionality to the language that would otherwise require more code.*

Sample: ConstructorsSample\Flavor.h

```
#pragma once


namespace Desserts
{

    enum class Flavor
    {

        None,

        Vanilla,

        Chocolate,

        Strawberry

    };


    inline Flavor operator|=(Flavor a, Flavor b)
    {

        return static_cast<Flavor>(static_cast<int>(a) | static_cast<int>(b));

    }
```

```cpp
inline const wchar_t* GetFlavorString(Flavor flavor)
{
    switch (flavor)
    {
    case Desserts::Flavor::None:
        return L"No Flavor Selected";
        break;
    case Desserts::Flavor::Vanilla:
        return L"Vanilla";
        break;
    case Desserts::Flavor::Chocolate:
        return L"Chocolate";
        break;
    case Desserts::Flavor::Strawberry:
        return L"Strawberry";
        break;
    default:
        return L"Unknown";
        break;
    }
}
}
```

Sample: ConstructorsSample\Toppings.h

```cpp
#pragma once
#include <string>
#include <sstream>


namespace Desserts
{
    class Toppings
    {
    public:

        enum ToppingsList : unsigned int
```

```cpp
    {
        None =                          0x00,

        HotFudge =              0x01,

        RaspberrySyrup =    0x02,

        CrushedWalnuts =    0x04,

        WhippedCream =          0x08,

        Cherry =                0x10
    } m_toppings;


    Toppings(void) :

        m_toppings(None),

        m_toppingsString()

    {

    }


    Toppings(ToppingsList toppings) :

        m_toppings(toppings),

        m_toppingsString()

    {

    }


    ~Toppings(void)

    {

    }


    const wchar_t* GetString(void)

    {

        if (m_toppings == None)

        {

            m_toppingsString = L"None";

            return m_toppingsString.c_str();

        }

        bool addSpace = false;

        std::wstringstream wstrstream;

        if (m_toppings & HotFudge)
```

```cpp
    {
        if (addSpace)
        {
            wstrstream << L" ";
        }
        wstrstream << L"Hot Fudge";
        addSpace = true;
    }

    if (m_toppings & RaspberrySyrup)
    {
        if (addSpace)
        {
            wstrstream << L" ";
        }
        wstrstream << L"Raspberry Syrup";
        addSpace = true;
    }

    if (m_toppings & CrushedWalnuts)
    {
        if (addSpace)
        {
            wstrstream << L" ";
        }
        wstrstream << L"Crushed Walnuts";
        addSpace = true;
    }

    if (m_toppings & WhippedCream)
    {
        if (addSpace)
        {
            wstrstream << L" ";
        }
        wstrstream << L"Whipped Cream";
        addSpace = true;
    }
```

```cpp
                    if (m_toppings & Cherry)
                    {
                        if (addSpace)
                        {
                            wstrstream << L" ";
                        }
                        wstrstream << L"Cherry";
                        addSpace = true;
                    }
                    m_toppingsString = std::wstring(wstrstream.str());
                    return m_toppingsString.c_str();
        }

    private:
        std::wstring                m_toppingsString;
    };


    inline Toppings operator&(Toppings a, unsigned int b)
    {
        a.m_toppings = static_cast<Toppings::ToppingsList>(static_cast<int>(a.m_toppings) &
b);
        return a;
    }



    inline Toppings::ToppingsList operator&(Toppings::ToppingsList a, unsigned int b)
    {
        auto val = static_cast<Toppings::ToppingsList>(static_cast<unsigned int>(a) & b);
        return val;
    }



    inline Toppings::ToppingsList operator|(Toppings::ToppingsList a, Toppings::ToppingsList
b)
    {
        return static_cast<Toppings::ToppingsList>(static_cast<int>(a) | static_cast<int>
(b));
    }
```

```
        inline Toppings operator|(Toppings a, Toppings::ToppingsList b)
        {
            a.m_toppings = static_cast<Toppings::ToppingsList>(static_cast<int>(a.m_toppings) |
static_cast<int>(b));

            return a;
        }
}
```

Sample: ConstructorsSample\IceCreamSundae.h

```cpp
#pragma once

#include "Flavor.h"

#include "Toppings.h"

#include <string>


namespace Desserts
{
    class IceCreamSundae
    {
    public:
        IceCreamSundae(void);

        IceCreamSundae(Flavor flavor);

        explicit IceCreamSundae(Toppings::ToppingsList toppings);

        IceCreamSundae(const IceCreamSundae& other);
        IceCreamSundae& operator=(const IceCreamSundae& other);

        IceCreamSundae(IceCreamSundae&& other);
        IceCreamSundae& operator=(IceCreamSundae&& other);


        ~IceCreamSundae(void);


        void AddTopping(Toppings::ToppingsList topping);


        void RemoveTopping(Toppings::ToppingsList topping);
```

```cpp
        void ChangeFlavor(Flavor flavor);

        const wchar_t* GetSundaeDescription(void);


    private:
        Flavor                  m_flavor;

        Toppings                m_toppings;

        std::wstring            m_description;
    };
}
```

Sample: ConstructorsSample\IceCreamSundae.cpp

```cpp
#include "IceCreamSundae.h"
#include <string>
#include <sstream>
#include <iostream>
#include <ostream>
#include <memory>

using namespace Desserts;
using namespace std;

IceCreamSundae::IceCreamSundae(void) :
    m_flavor(Flavor::None),
    m_toppings(Toppings::None),
    m_description()
{
    wcout << L"Default constructing IceCreamSundae(void)." <<
        endl;
}


IceCreamSundae::IceCreamSundae(Flavor flavor) :
    m_flavor(flavor),
    m_toppings(Toppings::None),
    m_description()
```

```cpp
{
    wcout << L"Conversion constructing IceCreamSundae(Flavor)." <<
        endl;
}


IceCreamSundae::IceCreamSundae(Toppings::ToppingsList toppings) :
    m_flavor(Flavor::None),
    m_toppings(toppings),
    m_description()
{
    wcout << L"Parameter constructing IceCreamSundae(\
                Toppings::ToppingsList)." << endl;
}


IceCreamSundae::IceCreamSundae(const IceCreamSundae& other) :
    m_flavor(other.m_flavor),
    m_toppings(other.m_toppings),
    m_description()
{
    wcout << L"Copy constructing IceCreamSundae." << endl;
}


IceCreamSundae& IceCreamSundae::operator=(const IceCreamSundae& other)
{
    wcout << L"Copy assigning IceCreamSundae." << endl;

    m_flavor = other.m_flavor;
    m_toppings = other.m_toppings;
    return *this;
}


IceCreamSundae::IceCreamSundae(IceCreamSundae&& other) :
    m_flavor(),
    m_toppings(),
    m_description()
```

```cpp
{
    wcout << L"Move constructing IceCreamSundae." << endl;

    *this = std::move(other);
}


IceCreamSundae& IceCreamSundae::operator=(IceCreamSundae&& other)
{
    wcout << L"Move assigning IceCreamSundae." << endl;


    if (this != &other)
    {
        m_flavor = std::move(other.m_flavor);
        m_toppings = std::move(other.m_toppings);
        m_description = std::move(other.m_description);
        other.m_flavor = Flavor::None;
        other.m_toppings = Toppings::None;
        other.m_description = std::wstring();
    }
    return *this;
}


IceCreamSundae::~IceCreamSundae(void)
{
    wcout << L"Destroying IceCreamSundae." << endl;
}


void IceCreamSundae::AddTopping(Toppings::ToppingsList topping)
{
    m_toppings = m_toppings | topping;
}


void IceCreamSundae::RemoveTopping(Toppings::ToppingsList topping)
{
    m_toppings = m_toppings & ~topping;
}
```

```cpp
void IceCreamSundae::ChangeFlavor(Flavor flavor)
{
    m_flavor = flavor;
}


const wchar_t* IceCreamSundae::GetSundaeDescription(void)
{
    wstringstream str;

    str << L"A " << GetFlavorString(m_flavor) <<
        L" sundae with the following toppings: " << m_toppings.GetString();

    m_description = wstring(str.str());

    return m_description.c_str();
}
```

Sample: ConstructorsSample\ConstructorsSample.cpp

```cpp
#include <iostream>
#include <ostream>
#include "IceCreamSundae.h"
#include "Flavor.h"
#include "Toppings.h"
#include "../pchar.h"


using namespace Desserts;
using namespace std;


typedef Desserts::Toppings::ToppingsList ToppingsList;


int _pmain(int /*argc*/, _pchar* /*argv*/[])
{
    const wchar_t* outputPrefixStr = L"Current Dessert: ";


    IceCreamSundae s1 = Flavor::Vanilla;


    wcout << outputPrefixStr << s1.GetSundaeDescription() << endl;

    s1.AddTopping(ToppingsList::HotFudge);
```

```
        wcout << outputPrefixStr << s1.GetSundaeDescription() << endl;

        s1.AddTopping(ToppingsList::Cherry);

        wcout << outputPrefixStr << s1.GetSundaeDescription() << endl;

        s1.AddTopping(ToppingsList::CrushedWalnuts);

        wcout << outputPrefixStr << s1.GetSundaeDescription() << endl;

        s1.AddTopping(ToppingsList::WhippedCream);

        wcout << outputPrefixStr << s1.GetSundaeDescription() << endl;

        s1.RemoveTopping(ToppingsList::CrushedWalnuts);

        wcout << outputPrefixStr << s1.GetSundaeDescription() << endl;


        wcout << endl <<
                L"Copy constructing s2 from s1." << endl;
        IceCreamSundae s2(s1);


        wcout << endl <<
                L"Copy assignment to s1 from s2." << endl;
        s1 = s2;


        wcout << endl <<
                L"Move constructing s3 from s1." << endl;
        IceCreamSundae s3(std::move(s1));


        wcout << endl <<
                L"Move assigning to s1 from s2." << endl;
        s1 = std::move(s2);


        return 0;

}
```

Chapter 6   Resource Acquisition is Initialization

What Is RAII?

RAII stands for "resource acquisition is initialization." RAII is a design pattern using C++ code to eliminate resource leaks. Resource leaks happen when a resource that your program acquired is not subsequently released. The most familiar example is a memory leak. Since C++ doesn't have a GC the way C# does, you need to be careful to ensure that dynamically allocated memory is freed. Otherwise, you will leak that memory. Resource leaks can also result in the inability to open a file because the file system thinks it's already open, the inability to obtain a lock in a multi-threaded program, or the inability to release a COM object.

How Does RAII Work?

RAII works because of three basic facts.

1. When an automatic storage duration object goes out of scope, its destructor runs.

2. When an exception occurs, all automatic duration objects that have been fully constructed since the last try-block began are destroyed in the reverse order they were created before any catch handler is invoked.

3. If you nest try-blocks, and none of the catch handlers of an inner try-block handles that type of exception, then the exception propagates to the outer try-block. All automatic duration objects that have been fully constructed within that outer try-block are then destroyed in reverse creation order before any catch handler is invoked, and so on, until something catches the exception or your program crashes.

RAII helps ensure that you release resources, without exceptions occurring, by simply using automatic storage duration objects that contain the resources. It is similar to the combination of the `System.IDisposable` interface along with the `using` statement in C#. Once execution leaves the current block, whether through successful execution or an exception, the resources are freed.

When it comes to exceptions, a key part to remember is that only fully constructed objects are destroyed. If you receive an exception in the midst of a constructor, and the last `try` block began outside that constructor, since the object isn't fully constructed, its destructor will not run.

This does not mean its member variables, which are objects, will not be destroyed. Any member variable objects that were fully constructed within the constructor before the exception occurred are fully constructed automatic duration objects. Thus, those member objects will be destroyed the same as any other fully constructed objects.

This is why you should always put dynamic allocations inside either `std::unique_ptr` or `std::shared_ptr`. Instances of those types become fully constructed objects when the allocation succeeds. Even if the constructor for the object you are creating fails further in, the `std::unique_ptr` resources will be freed by its destructor and the `std::shared_ptr` resources will have their reference count decremented and will be freed if the count becomes zero.

RAII isn't about `shared_ptr` and `unique_ptr` only, of course. It also applies to other resource types, such as a file object, where the acquisition is the opening of the file and the destructor ensures that the file is properly closed. This is a particularly good example since you only need to create that code right just once—when you write the class—rather than again and again, which is what you need to do if you write the close logic every place you have to open a file.

How Do I Use RAII?

RAII use is described by its name: Acquiring a dynamic resource should complete the initialization of an object. If you follow this one-resource-per-object pattern, then it is impossible to wind up with a resource leak. Either you will successfully acquire the resource, in which case the object that encapsulates it will finish construction and be subject to destruction, or the acquisition attempt will fail, in which case you did not acquire the resource; thus, there is no resource to release.

The destructor of an object that encapsulates a resource must release that resource. This, among other things, is one of the important reasons why destructors should never throw exceptions, except those they catch and handle within themselves.

If the destructor threw an uncaught exception, then, to quote Bjarne Stroustrup, "All kinds of bad things are likely to happen because the basic rules of the standard library and the language itself will be violated. Don't do it."

As he said, *don't do it*. Make sure you know what exceptions, if any, everything you call in your destructors could throw so you can ensure that you handle them properly.

Now you might be thinking that if you follow this pattern, you will end up writing a ton of classes. You will occasionally write an extra class here and there, but you aren't likely to write too many because of smart pointers. Smart pointers are objects too. Most types of dynamic resources can be put into at least one of the existing smart pointer classes. When you put a resource acquisition inside a suitable smart pointer, if the acquisition succeeds, then that smart pointer object will be fully constructed. If an exception occurs, then the smart pointer object's destructor will be called, and the resource will be freed.

There are several important smart pointer types. Let's have a look at them.

std::unique_ptr

The unique pointer, `std::unique_ptr`, is designed to hold a pointer to a dynamically allocated object. You should use this type only when you want one pointer to the object to exist. It is a template class that takes a mandatory and an optional template argument. The mandatory argument is the type of the pointer it will hold. For instance `auto result = std::unique_ptr<int>(new int());` will create a unique pointer that contains an `int*`. The optional argument is the type of deleter. We see how to write a deleter in a coming sample. Typically, you can avoid specifying a deleter since the `default_deleter`, which is provided for you if no deleter is specified, covers almost every case you can imagine.

A class that has `std::unique_ptr` as a member variable cannot have a default copy constructor. Copy semantics are disabled for `std::unique_ptr`. If you want a copy constructor in a class that has a unique pointer, you must write it. You should also write an overload for the copy operator. Normally, you want `std::shared_ptr` in that case.

However, you might have something like an array of data. You may also want any copy of the class to create a copy of the data as it exists at that time. In that case, a unique pointer with a custom copy constructor could be the right choice.

`std::unique_ptr` is defined in the `<memory>` header file.

`std::unique_ptr` has four member functions of interest.

The `get` member function returns the stored pointer. If you need to call a function that you need to pass the contained pointer to, use `get` to retrieve a copy of the pointer.

The `release` member function also returns the stored pointer, but `release` invalidates the unique_ptr in the process by replacing the stored pointer with a null pointer. If you have a function where you want to create a dynamic object and then return it, while still maintaining exception safety, use `std:unique_ptr` to store the dynamically created object, and then return the result of calling `release`. This gives you exception safety while allowing you to return the dynamic object without destroying it with the `std::unique_ptr`'s destructor when the control exits from the function upon returning the released pointer value at the end.

The `swap` member function allows two unique pointers to exchange their stored pointers, so if `A` is holding a pointer to `x`, and `B` is holding a pointer to `y`, the result of calling `A::swap(B);` is that `A` will now hold a pointer to `y`, and `B` will hold a pointer to `x`. The deleters for each will also be swapped, so if you have a custom deleter for either or both of the unique pointers, be assured that each will retain its associated deleter.

The `reset` member function causes the object pointed to by the stored pointer, if any, to be destroyed in most cases. If the current stored pointer is null, then nothing is destroyed. If you pass in a pointer to the object that the current stored pointer points to, then nothing is destroyed. You can choose to pass in a new pointer, `nullptr`, or to call the function with no parameters. If you pass in a new pointer, then that new object is stored. If you pass in `nullptr`, then the unique pointer will store null. Calling the function with no parameters is the same as calling it with `nullptr`.

std::shared_ptr

The shared pointer, std::shared_ptr, is designed to hold a pointer to a dynamically allocated object and to keep a reference count for it. It is not magic; if you create two shared pointers and pass them each a pointer to the same object, you will end up with two shared pointers—each with a reference count of 1, not 2. The first one that is destroyed will release the underlying resource, giving catastrophic results when you try to use the other one or when the other one is destroyed and tries to release the already released underlying resource.

To use the shared pointer properly, create one instance with an object pointer and then create all other shared pointers for that object from an existing, valid shared pointer for that object. This ensures a common reference count, so the resource will have a proper lifetime. Let's look at a quick sample to see the right and wrong ways to create shared_ptr objects.

Sample: SharedPtrSample\SharedPtrSample.cpp

```cpp
#include <memory>

#include <iostream>

#include <ostream>

#include "../pchar.h"


using namespace std;


struct TwoInts

{

    TwoInts(void) : A(), B() { }

    TwoInts(int a, int b) : A(a), B(b) { }

    int A;

    int B;

};


wostream& operator<<(wostream& stream, TwoInts* v)

{

    stream << v->A << L" " << v->B;

    return stream;

}


int _pmain(int /*argc*/, _pchar* /*argv*/[])
```

```cpp
{
    //// Bad: results in double free.
    //try
    //{
    //    TwoInts* p_i = new TwoInts(10, 20);

    //    auto sp1 = shared_ptr<TwoInts>(p_i);
    //    auto sp2 = shared_ptr<TwoInts>(p_i);
    //    p_i = nullptr;

    //    wcout << L"sp1 count is " << sp1.use_count() << L"." << endl <<
    //        L"sp2 count is " << sp2.use_count() << L"." << endl;
    //}
    //catch(exception& e)
    //{
    //    wcout << L"There was an exception." << endl;
    //    wcout << e.what() << endl << endl;
    //}
    //catch(...)
    //{
    //    wcout << L"There was an exception due to a double free " <<
    //        L"because we tried freeing p_i twice!" << endl;
    //}


    // This is one right way to create shared_ptrs.
    {
        auto sp1 = shared_ptr<TwoInts>(new TwoInts(10, 20));
        auto sp2 = shared_ptr<TwoInts>(sp1);

        wcout << L"sp1 count is " << sp1.use_count() << L"." << endl <<
            L"sp2 count is " << sp2.use_count() << L"." << endl;

        wcout << L"sp1 value is " << sp1 << L"." << endl <<
            L"sp2 value is " << sp2 << L"." << endl;

    }
```

```
// This is another right way. The std::make_shared function takes the
// type as its template argument, and then the argument value(s) to the
// constructor you want as its parameters, and it automatically
// constructs the object for you. This is usually more memory-
// efficient, as the reference count can be stored with the
// shared_ptr's pointed-to object at the time of the object's creation.
{
    auto sp1 = make_shared<TwoInts>(10, 20);
    auto sp2 = shared_ptr<TwoInts>(sp1);

    wcout << L"sp1 count is " << sp1.use_count() << L"." << endl <<
        L"sp2 count is " << sp2.use_count() << L"." << endl;

    wcout << L"sp1 value is " << sp1 << L"." << endl <<
        L"sp2 value is " << sp2 << L"." << endl;
}


    return 0;
}
```

`std::shared_ptr` is defined in the <memory> header file.

`std::shared_ptr` has five member functions of interest.

The `get` member function works the same as the `std::unique_ptr::get` member function.

The `use_count` member function returns a `long`, which tells you what the current reference count for the target object is. This does not include weak references.

The `unique` member function returns a `bool`, informing you whether this particular shared pointer is the sole owner of the target object.

The `swap` member function works the same as the `std::unique_ptr::swap` member function, with the addition that the reference counts for the resources stay the same.

The `reset` member function decrements the reference count for the underlying resource and destroys it if the resource count becomes zero. If a pointer to an object is passed in, the shared pointer will store it and begin a new reference count for that pointer. If `nullptr` is passed in, or if no parameter is passed, then the shared pointer will store null.

std::make_shared

The `std::make_shared` template function is a convenient way to construct an initial `std::shared_ptr`. As we saw previously in **SharedPtrSample**, you pass the type as the template argument and then simply pass in the arguments, if any, for the desired constructor. std::make_shared will construct a heap instance of the template argument object type and make it into a `std::shared_ptr`. You can then pass that `std::shared_ptr` as an argument to the `std::shared_ptr` constructor to create more references to that shared object.

`ComPtr` in WRL for Metro-Style Apps

The Windows Runtime Template Library (WRL) provides a smart pointer named `ComPtr` within the `Microsoft::WRL` namespace for use with COM objects in Windows 8 Metro-style applications. The pointer is found in the <wrl/client.h> header, as part of the Windows SDK (minimum version 8.0).

Most of the operating system functionality that you can use in Metro-style applications is exposed by the Windows Runtime ("WinRT"). WinRT objects provide their own automatic reference counting functionality for object creation and destruction. Some system functionality, such as Direct3D, requires you to directly use and manipulate it through classic COM. `ComPtr` handles COM's `IUnknown`-based reference counting for you. It also provides convenient wrappers for `QueryInterface` and includes other functionality that is useful for smart pointers.

The two member functions you typically use are `As` to get a different interface for the underlying COM object and `Get` to take an interface pointer to the underlying COM object that the ComPtr holds (this is the equivalent of `std::unique_ptr::get`).

Sometimes you will use `Detach`, which works the same way as `std::unique_ptr::release` but has a different name because *release* in COM implies decrementing the reference count and `Detach` does not do that.

You might use `ReleaseAndGetAddressOf` for situations where you have an existing `ComPtr` that could already hold a COM object and you want to replace it with a new COM object of the same type. `ReleaseAndGetAddressOf` does the same thing as the `GetAddressOf` member function, but `it` first releases its underlying interface, if any.

Exceptions in C++

Unlike .NET, where all exceptions derive from `System.Exception` and have guaranteed methods and properties, C++ exceptions are not required to derive from anything; nor are they even required to be class types. In C++, `throw L"Hello World!";` is perfectly acceptable to the compiler as is `throw 5;`. Basically, exceptions can be anything.

That said, many C++ programmers will be unhappy to see an exception that does not derive from `std::exception` (found in the `<exception>` header). Deriving all exceptions from `std::exception` provides a way to catch exceptions of unknown type and retrieve information from them via the `what` member function before re-throwing them. `std::exception::what` takes no parameters and returns a `const char*` string, which you can view or log so you know what caused the exception.

There is no stack trace—not counting the stack-trace capabilities your debugger provides—with C++ exceptions. Because automatic duration objects within the scope of the try-block that catches the exception are automatically destroyed before the appropriate catch handler, if any, is activated, you do not have the luxury of examining the data that may have caused the exception. All you have to work with initially is the message from the `what` member function.

If it is easy to recreate the conditions that led to the exception, you can set a breakpoint and rerun the program, allowing you to step through execution of the trouble area and possibly spot the issue. Because that is not always possible, it is important to be as precise as you can with the error message.

When deriving from `std::exception`, you should make sure to override the `what` member function to provide a useful error message that will help you and other developers diagnose what went wrong.

Some programmers use a variant of a rule stating that you should always throw `std::exception`-derived exceptions. Remembering that the entry point (`main` or `wmain`) returns an integer, these programmers will throw `std::exception`-derived exceptions when their code can recover, but will simply throw a well-defined integer value if the failure is unrecoverable. The entry-point code will be wrapped in a try-block that has a catch for an `int`. The catch handler will return the caught `int` value. On most systems, a return value of 0 from a program means success. Any other value means failure.

If there is a catastrophic failure, then throwing a well-defined integer value other than 0 can help provide some meaning. Unless you are working on a project where this is the preferred style, you should stick to `std::exception`-derived exceptions, since they let programs handle exceptions using a simple logging system to record messages from exceptions not handled, and they perform any cleanup that is safe. Throwing something that doesn't derive from `std::exception` would interfere with these error-logging mechanisms.

One last thing to note is that C#'s `finally` construct has no equivalent in C++. The RAII idiom, when properly implemented, makes it unnecessary since everything will have been cleaned up.

C++ Standard Library Exceptions

We've already discussed `std::exception`, but there are more types than that available in the standard library, and there is additional functionality to explore. Let's look at the functionality from the `<exception>` header file first.

The `std::terminate` function, by default, lets you crash out of any application. It should be used sparingly, since calling it rather than throwing an exception will bypass all normal exception handling mechanisms. If you wish, you can write a custom terminate function without parameters and return values. An example of this will be seen in **ExceptionsSample**, which is coming.

To set the custom terminate, you call `std::set_terminate` and pass it the address of the function. You can change the custom terminate handler at any time; the last function set is what will be called in the event of either a call to `std::terminate` or an unhandled exception. The default handler calls the abort function from the `<cstdlib>` header file.

The `<stdexcept>` header provides a rudimentary framework for exceptions. It defines two classes that inherit from `std::exception`. Those two classes serve as the parent class for several other classes.

The `std::runtime_error` class is the parent class for exceptions thrown by the runtime or due to a mistake in a C++ Standard Library function. Its children are the `std::overflow_error` class, the `std::range_error` class, and the `std::underflow_error` class.

The `std::logic_error` class is the parent class for exceptions thrown due to programmer error. Its children are the `std::domain_error` class, the `std::invalid_argument` class, the `std::length_error` class, and the `std::out_of_range` class.

You can derive from these classes or create your own exception classes. Coming up with a good exception hierarchy is a difficult task. On one hand, you want exceptions that will be specific enough that you can handle all exceptions based on your knowledge at build-time. On the other hand, you do not want an exception class for each error that could occur. Your code would end up bloated and unwieldy, not to mention the waste of time writing catch handlers for every exception class.

Spend time at a whiteboard, or with a pen and paper, or however you want thinking about the exception tree your application should have.

The following sample contains a class called `InvalidArgumentExceptionBase`, which is used as the parent of a template class called `InvalidArgumentException`. The combination of a base class, which can be caught with one exception handler, and a template class, which allows us to customize the output diagnostics based on the type of the parameter, is one option for balancing between specialization and code bloat.

The template class might seem confusing right now; we will be discussing templates in an upcoming chapter, at which point anything currently unclear should clear up.

Sample: ExceptionsSample\InvalidArgumentException.h

```cpp
#pragma once

#include <exception>

#include <stdexcept>

#include <string>

#include <sstream>


namespace CppForCsExceptions

{

    class InvalidArgumentExceptionBase :

        public std::invalid_argument

    {

    public:

        InvalidArgumentExceptionBase(void) :

            std::invalid_argument("") { }


        virtual ~InvalidArgumentExceptionBase(void) throw() { }


        virtual const char* what(void) const throw() override = 0;

    };


    template <class T>

    class InvalidArgumentException :

        public InvalidArgumentExceptionBase

    {

    public:

        inline InvalidArgumentException(

            const char* className,

            const char* functionSignature,

            const char* parameterName,

            T parameterValue

            );
```

```cpp
        inline virtual ~InvalidArgumentException(void) throw();


        inline virtual const char* what(void) const throw() override;

    private:

        std::string m_whatMessage;
    };


    template<class T>
    InvalidArgumentException<T>::InvalidArgumentException(
        const char* className,
        const char* functionSignature,
        const char* parameterName,
        T parameterValue) : InvalidArgumentExceptionBase(),
        m_whatMessage()
    {

        std::stringstream msg;
        msg << className << "::" << functionSignature <<
            " - parameter '" << parameterName << "' had invalid value '" <<
            parameterValue << "'.";
        m_whatMessage = std::string(msg.str());
    }


    template<class T>
    InvalidArgumentException<T>::~InvalidArgumentException(void) throw()
    { }


    template<class T>
    const char* InvalidArgumentException<T>::what(void) const throw()
    {

        return m_whatMessage.c_str();

    }

}
```

Sample: ExceptionsSample\ExceptionsSample.cpp

```cpp
#include <iostream>
```

```cpp
#include <ostream>
#include <memory>
#include <exception>
#include <stdexcept>
#include <typeinfo>
#include <algorithm>
#include <cstdlib>
#include "InvalidArgumentException.h"
#include "../pchar.h"

using namespace CppForCsExceptions;
using namespace std;

class ThrowClass
{
public:
    ThrowClass(void)
        : m_shouldThrow(false)
    {
        wcout << L"Constructing ThrowClass." << endl;
    }


    explicit ThrowClass(bool shouldThrow)
        : m_shouldThrow(shouldThrow)
    {
        wcout << L"Constructing ThrowClass. shouldThrow = " <<
            (shouldThrow ? L"true." : L"false.") << endl;
        if (shouldThrow)
        {
            throw InvalidArgumentException<const char*>(
                "ThrowClass",
                "ThrowClass(bool shouldThrow)",
                "shouldThrow",
                "true"
                );
```

```cpp
                }
        }


        ~ThrowClass(void)

        {

                wcout << L"Destroying ThrowClass." << endl;

        }


        const wchar_t* GetShouldThrow(void) const

        {

                return (m_shouldThrow ? L"True" : L"False");

        }


private:

        bool        m_shouldThrow;
};


class RegularClass

{

public:

        RegularClass(void)

        {

                wcout << L"Constructing RegularClass." << endl;

        }

        ~RegularClass(void)

        {

                wcout << L"Destroying RegularClass." << endl;

        }
};


class ContainStuffClass

{

public:

        ContainStuffClass(void) :

                m_regularClass(new RegularClass()),
```

```cpp
        m_throwClass(new ThrowClass())
    {
        wcout << L"Constructing ContainStuffClass." << endl;
    }


    ContainStuffClass(const ContainStuffClass& other) :
        m_regularClass(new RegularClass(*other.m_regularClass)),
        m_throwClass(other.m_throwClass)
    {
        wcout << L"Copy constructing ContainStuffClass." << endl;
    }


    ~ContainStuffClass(void)
    {
        wcout << L"Destroying ContainStuffClass." << endl;
    }


    const wchar_t* GetString(void) const
    {
        return L"I'm a ContainStuffClass.";
    }


private:

    unique_ptr<RegularClass>        m_regularClass;
    shared_ptr<ThrowClass>          m_throwClass;
};


void TerminateHandler(void)
{
    wcout << L"Terminating due to unhandled exception." << endl;

    // If you call abort (from <cstdlib>), the program will exit
    // abnormally. It will also exit abnormally if you do not call
    // anything to cause it to exit from this method.
```

```cpp
        abort();

        //// If you were instead to call exit(0) (also from <cstdlib>),
        //// then your program would exit as though nothing had
        //// gone wrong. This is bad because something did go wrong.
        //// I present this so you know that it is possible for
        //// a program to throw an uncaught exception and still
        //// exit in a way that isn't interpreted as a crash, since
        //// you may need to find out why a program keeps abruptly
        //// exiting yet isn't crashing. This would be one such cause
        //// for that.
        //exit(0);
}

int _pmain(int /*argc*/, _pchar* /*argv*/[])
{
        // Set a custom handler for std::terminate. Note that this handler
        // won't run unless you run it from a command prompt. The debugger
        // will intercept the unhandled exception and will present you with
        // debugging options when you run it from Visual Studio.
        set_terminate(&TerminateHandler);

        try
        {
                ContainStuffClass cSC;
                wcout << cSC.GetString() << endl;

                ThrowClass tC(false);
                wcout << L"tC should throw? " << tC.GetShouldThrow() << endl;

                tC = ThrowClass(true);
                wcout << L"tC should throw? " << tC.GetShouldThrow() << endl;
        }
        // One downside to using templates for exceptions is that you need a
        // catch handler for each specialization, unless you have a base
```

```cpp
    // class they all inherit from, that is. To avoid catching
    // other std::invalid_argument exceptions, we created an abstract
    // class called InvalidArgumentExceptionBase, which serves solely to
    // act as the base class for all specializations of
    // InvalidArgumentException<T>. Now we can catch them all, if desired,
    // without needing a catch handler for each. If you wanted to, however,
    // you could still have a handler for a particular specialization.
    catch (InvalidArgumentExceptionBase& e)
    {
        wcout << L"Caught '" << typeid(e).name() << L"'." << endl <<
            L"Message: " << e.what() << endl;
    }

    // Catch anything derived from std::exception that doesn't already
    // have a specialized handler. Since you don't know what this is, you
    // should catch it, log it, and re-throw it.
    catch (std::exception& e)
    {
        wcout << L"Caught '" << typeid(e).name() << L"'." << endl <<
            L"Message: " << e.what() << endl;
        // Just a plain throw statement like this is a re-throw.
        throw;
    }

    // This next catch catches everything, regardless of type. Like
    // catching System.Exception, you should only catch this to
    // re-throw it.
    catch (...)
    {
        wcout << L"Caught unknown exception type." << endl;
        throw;
    }


    // This will cause our custom terminate handler to run.
    wcout << L"tC should throw? " <<
        ThrowClass(true).GetShouldThrow() << endl;
```

```
    return 0;
}
```

Though I mention it in the comments, I just wanted to point out again that you will not see the custom terminate function run unless you run this sample from a command prompt. If you run it in Visual Studio, the debugger will intercept the program and orchestrate its own termination after giving you a chance to examine the state to see if you can determine what went wrong. Also, note that this program will always crash. This is by design since it allows you to see the terminate handler in action.

Chapter 7   Pointers, References, and Const-Correctness

Pointer Overview

A pointer is nothing more than a variable that holds a memory address. When used properly, a pointer holds a valid memory address that contains an object, which is compatible with the type of the pointer. Like references in C#, all pointers in a particular execution environment have the same size, regardless of the type of data the pointer points to. For example, when a program is compiled for and run on a 32-bit operating system, a pointer will typically be 4 bytes (32 bits).

Pointers can point to any memory address. You can, and frequently will, have pointers to objects that are on the stack. You can also have pointers to static objects, to thread local objects, and, of course, to dynamic (i.e., heap allocated) objects. When programmers with only a passing familiarity with pointers think of them, it's usually in the context of dynamic objects.

Because of potential leaks, you should *never* allocate dynamic memory outside of a smart pointer. The C++ Standard Library provides two smart pointers that you should consider: `std::shared_ptr` and `std::unique_ptr`.

By putting dynamic duration objects inside one of these, you guarantee that when the `std::unique_ptr`, or the last `std::shared_ptr` that contains a pointer to that memory goes out of scope, the memory will be properly freed with the correct version of delete (`delete` or `delete[]`) so it won't leak. That's the RAII pattern from the previous chapter in action.

Only two things can happen when you do RAII right with smart pointers: The allocation succeeds, and therefore the memory will be properly freed when the smart pointer goes out of scope or the allocation fails, in which case there was no memory allocated and thus no leak. In practice, the last situation should be quite rare on modern PCs and servers due to their large memory and their provision of virtual memory.

If you don't use smart pointers, you're just asking for a memory leak. Any exception between allocating the memory with `new` or `new[]` and freeing the memory with `delete` or `delete[]` will likely result in a memory leak. If you aren't careful, you could accidentally use a pointer that was already deleted, but was not set equal to `nullptr`. You would then be accessing some random location in memory and treating it like it's a valid pointer.

The best thing that could happen in that case is for your program to crash. If it doesn't, then you're corrupting data in strange, unknown ways and possibly saving those corruptions to a database or pushing them across the web. You could be opening the door to security problems too. So use smart pointers and let the language handle memory-management issues for you.

Const Pointer

A const pointer takes the form `someClass* const someClass2 = &someClass1;`. In other words, the `*` comes before `const`. The result is that the pointer itself cannot point to anything else, but the data the pointer points at remains mutable. This is not likely to be very useful in most situations.

Pointer to Const

A pointer to const takes the form `const SomeClass* someClass2 = &someClass1;`. In this case the `*` comes after `const`. The result is that the pointer can point to other things, but you cannot modify the data it points to. This is a common way to declare parameters that you simply want to inspect without modifying their data.

Const Pointer to Const

A const pointer to const takes the form `const SomeClass* const someClass2 = &someClass1;`. Here, the `*` is sandwiched between two `const` keywords. The result is that the pointer cannot point to anything else, and you cannot modify the data it points to.

Const-correctness and Const Member Functions

Const-correctness refers to using the `const` keyword to decorate both parameters and functions so the presence or absence of the `const` keyword properly conveys any potential side effects. You can mark a member function `const` by putting the `const` keyword after the declaration of the function's parameters.

For example, `int GetSomeInt(void) const;` declares a const member function—a member function that does not modify the data of the object it belongs to. The compiler will enforce this guarantee. It will also enforce the guarantee that when you pass an object into a function that takes it as const, that function cannot call any non-const member functions of that object.

Designing your program to adhere to const-correctness is easier when you start doing it from the beginning. When you adhere to const-correctness, it becomes easier to use multithreading, since you know exactly which member functions have side effects. It's also easier to track down bugs related to invalid data states. Others who are collaborating with you on a project will also be aware of potential changes to the class' data when they call certain member functions.

The * & and -> Operators

When working with pointers, including smart pointers, three operators are of interest: *, &, and ->.

The indirection operator, *, de-references a pointer, meaning you work with the data that is pointed to, instead of the pointer itself. For the next few paragraphs, let's assume that `p_someInt` is a valid pointer to an integer with no const qualifications.

The statement `p_someInt = 5000000;` would not assign the value 5000000 to the integer that is pointed to. Instead, it would set the pointer to point to the memory address 5000000, 0X004C4B40 on a 32-bit system. What is at memory address 0X004C4B40? Who knows? It could be your integer, but chances are it is something else. If you are lucky, it is an invalid address. The next time you try to use `p_someInt` properly, your program will crash. If it is a valid data address though, then you will likely corrupt data.

The statement `*p_someInt = 5000000;` will assign the value 5000000 to the integer pointed to by `p_someInt`. This is the indirection operator in action; it takes `p_someInt` and replaces it with an L-value that represents the data at the address pointed to (we'll discuss L-values soon).

The address-of operator, &, fetches the address of a variable or a function. This allows you to create a pointer to a local object, which you can pass to a function that wants a pointer. You don't even need to create a local pointer to do that; you can simply use your local variable with the address-of operator in front of it as the argument, and everything will work just fine.

Pointers to functions are similar to delegate instances in C#. Given this function declaration: `double GetValue(int idx);` this would be the right function pointer: `double (*SomeFunctionPtr)(int);`.

If your function returned a pointer, say like this: `int* GetIntPtr(void);` then this would be the right function pointer: `int* (*SomeIntPtrDelegate)(void);`. Don't let the double asterisks bother you; just remember the first set of parentheses around the * and function pointer name so the compiler properly interprets this as a function pointer rather than a function declaration.

The -> member access operator is what you use to access class members when you have a pointer to a class instance. It functions as a combination of the indirection operator and the . member access operator. So `p_someClassInstance->SetValue(10);` and `(*p_someClassInstance).SetValue(10);` both do the same thing.

L-values and R-values

It wouldn't be C++ if we didn't talk about L-values and R-values at least briefly. L-values are so called because they traditionally appear on the left side of an equal sign. In other words, they are values that can be assigned to—those which will survive the evaluation of the current expression. The most familiar type of L-value is a variable, but it also includes the result of calling a function that returns an L-value reference.

R-values traditionally appear on the right side of the equation or, perhaps more accurately, they are values that could not appear on the left. They are things such as constants, or the result of evaluating an equation. For example, a + b where a and b might be L-values, but the result of adding them together is an R-value, or the return value of a function that returns anything other than void or an L-value reference.

References

References act just like non-pointer variables. Once a reference is initialized, it cannot refer to another object. You also must initialize a reference where you declare it. If your functions take references rather than objects, you will not incur the cost of a copy construction. Since the reference refers to the object, changes to it are changes to the object itself.

Just like pointers, you can also have a const reference. Unless you need to modify the object, you should use const references since they provide compiler checks to ensure that you aren't mutating the object when you think you aren't.

There are two types of references: L-value references and R-value references. An L-value reference is marked by an `&` appended to the type name (e.g., `SomeClass&`), whereas an R-value reference is marked by an `&&` appended to the type name (e.g., `SomeClass&&`). For the most part, they act the same; the main difference is that the R-value reference is extremely important to move semantics.

Pointer and Reference Sample

The following sample shows pointer and reference usage with explanations in the comments.

Sample: PointerSample\PointerSample.cpp

```cpp
#include <memory>
//// See the comment to the first use of assert() in _pmain below.
//#define NDEBUG 1
#include <cassert>
#include "../pchar.h"


using namespace std;


void SetValueToZero(int& value)
{
    value = 0;
}


void SetValueToZero(int* value)
{
    *value = 0;
}


int _pmain(int /*argc*/, _pchar* /*argv*/[])
{
    int value = 0;

    const int intArrCount = 20;
    // Create a pointer to int.
    int* p_intArr = new int[intArrCount];

    // Create a const pointer to int.
    int* const cp_intArr = p_intArr;

    // These two statements are fine since we can modify the data that a
```

```cpp
// const pointer points to.
// Set all elements to 5.
uninitialized_fill_n(cp_intArr, intArrCount, 5);
// Sets the first element to zero.
*cp_intArr = 0;


//// This statement is illegal because we cannot modify what a const
//// pointer points to.
//cp_intArr = nullptr;


// Create a pointer to const int.
const int* pc_intArr = nullptr;


// This is fine because we can modify what a pointer to const points
// to.
pc_intArr = p_intArr;


// Make sure we "use" pc_intArr.
value = *pc_intArr;


//// This statement is illegal since we cannot modify the data that a
//// pointer to const points to.
//*pc_intArr = 10;


const int* const cpc_intArr = p_intArr;


//// These two statements are illegal because we cannot modify
//// what a const pointer to const points to or the data it
//// points to.
//cpc_intArr = p_intArr;
//*cpc_intArr = 20;


// Make sure we "use" cpc_intArr.
value = *cpc_intArr;
```

```cpp
    *p_intArr = 6;

    SetValueToZero(*p_intArr);

    // From <cassert>, this macro will display a diagnostic message if the
    // expression in parentheses evaluates to anything other than zero.
    // Unlike the _ASSERTE macro, this will run during Release builds. To
    // disable it, define NDEBUG before including the <cassert> header.
    assert(*p_intArr == 0);

    *p_intArr = 9;

    int& r_first = *p_intArr;

    SetValueToZero(r_first);

    assert(*p_intArr == 0);

    const int& cr_first = *p_intArr;

    //// This statement is illegal because cr_first is a const reference,
    //// but SetValueToZero does not take a const reference, only a
    //// non-const reference, which makes sense considering it wants to
    //// modify the value.
    //SetValueToZero(cr_first);

    value = cr_first;

    // We can initialize a pointer using the address-of operator.
    // Just be wary because local non-static variables become
    // invalid when you exit their scope, so any pointers to them
    // become invalid.
    int* p_firstElement = &r_first;

    *p_firstElement = 10;
```

```cpp
    SetValueToZero(*p_firstElement);


    assert(*p_firstElement == 0);


    // This will call the SetValueToZero(int*) overload because we
    // are using the address-of operator to turn the reference into
    // a pointer.
    SetValueToZero(&r_first);


    *p_intArr = 3;


    SetValueToZero(&(*p_intArr));


    assert(*p_firstElement == 0);


    // Create a function pointer. Notice how we need to put the
    // variable name in parentheses with a * before it.
    void (*FunctionPtrToSVTZ)(int&) = nullptr;


    // Set the function pointer to point to SetValueToZero. It picks
    // the correct overload automatically.
    FunctionPtrToSVTZ = &SetValueToZero;


    *p_intArr = 20;


    // Call the function pointed to by FunctionPtrToSVTZ, i.e.
    // SetValueToZero(int&).
    FunctionPtrToSVTZ(*p_intArr);


    assert(*p_intArr == 0);


    *p_intArr = 50;


    // We can also call a function pointer like this. This is
```

```cpp
    // closer to what is actually happening behind the scenes;
    // FunctionPtrToSVTZ is being de-referenced with the result
    // being the function that is pointed to, which we then
    // call using the value(s) specified in the second set of
    // parentheses, i.e. *p_intArr here.
    (*FunctionPtrToSVTZ)(*p_intArr);


    assert(*p_intArr == 0);


    // Make sure that we get value set to 0 so we can "use" it.
    *p_intArr = 0;
    value = *p_intArr;


    // Delete the p_intArray using the delete[] operator since it is a
    // dynamic p_intArray.
    delete[] p_intArr;
    p_intArr = nullptr;
    return value;
}
```

Volatile

I mention volatile only to caution against using it. Like const, a variable can be declared volatile. You can even have a const volatile; the two are not mutually exclusive.

Here's the thing about volatile: It likely does not mean what you think it means. For example, it is not good for multithreaded programming. The actual use case for volatile is extremely narrow. Chances are, if you put the volatile qualifier on a variable, you are doing something horribly wrong.

Eric Lippert, a member of the C# language team at Microsoft, described the use of volatile as, "A sign that you are doing something downright *crazy*: You're attempting to read and write the same value on two different threads without putting a lock in place." He's right, and his argument carries over perfectly into C++.

The use of volatile should be greeted with more skepticism than the use of goto. I say this because I can think of at least one valid general-purpose use of goto: breaking out of a deeply nested loop construct upon the completion of a non-exceptional condition. volatile, by contrast, is really only useful if you are writing a device driver or writing code for some type of ROM chip. On that point, you really should be thoroughly familiar with the ISO/IEC C++ Programming Language Standard itself, the hardware specs for the execution environment your code will be running in, and probably the ISO/IEC C Language Standard too.

 Note: You should also be familiar with assembly language for the target hardware, so you can look at code that is generated and make sure the compiler is generating correct code (PDF) for your use of volatile.

I have been ignoring the existence of the volatile keyword and shall continue to do so for the remainder of this book. This is perfectly safe, since:

- It's a language feature that doesn't come into play unless you actually use it.
- Its use can safely be avoided by virtually everyone.

One last note about volatile: The one effect it is very likely to produce is slower code. Once upon a time, people thought volatile produced the same result as atomicity. It doesn't. When properly implemented, atomicity guarantees that multiple threads and multiple processors cannot read and write an atomically accessed chunk of memory at the same time. The mechanisms for this are locks, mutexes, semaphores, fences, special processor instructions, and the like. The only thing volatile does is force the CPU to fetch a volatile variable from memory rather than use any value it might have cached in a register or on a stack. It is the memory fetching that slows everything down.

Chapter 8   Casting in C++

Overview

There are five different ways of casting variables. There is overlap between them, especially with the C-style cast and all other casts, but each has its use. It is good to learn them all, so you can use the best cast for your particular need rather than using any cast that happens to work. If you ever need a quick reference, I recommend this post on StackOverflow.

I'm not discussing implicit casting here for the simple reason that it's a basic concept with an almost infinite number of variations. If I write `float f = 10;` I've implicitly cast an integer to a float and stored its result in `f`. You can also implicitly cast an object of type B to a pointer to its base class A using the address-of operator or to a reference to its base class A by doing a normal assignment.

const_cast

The `const_cast` operator can add and remove `const` and `volatile`. Using it to add either of these attributes is fine. It's rare that you would, but if you do, you can.

Its ability to remove `const` is something you should never use in a C++ program except when you need to call a C-language function that doesn't abide by const-correctness but does not modify the object at all. If a function has a `const` parameter, and throws out the const-ness of it by using `const_cast`, the function is breaking the implied contract that it will not modify the parameter. So it's up to you as the author of that function to ensure that you are not going to modify the object; otherwise, you should not use `const` for the parameter since you will be modifying the object.

If you ever need to use `const_cast` and another cast operator on the same object, use `const_cast` last, since removing const-ness from an object could allow unintended changes to take place if you used a subsequent cast.

static_cast

The `static_cast` operator is useful for casting:

- Floating point types to integer types (producing a truncated result).
- Integer types to floating point types.
- Enum types to integer types.
- Integer types to enum types.
- Derived classes to base classes.
- A types to a derived type reference.
- A derived class pointer to a base class pointer.

In general, whenever casting fundamental types to other fundamental types, use `static_cast`. Typically, static_cast should be your first choice of casts, as it does all the checking it can do at compile-time, so you don't have added run-time checking to slow down your program.

dynamic_cast

The `dynamic_cast` operator is useful for casting through virtual inheritance. `static_cast` can cast from a derived class to a base class, whether the inheritance is virtual or not. Say, however, you are given an object of type A, but you know it is actually an object of type B—and that B inherits virtually from A. If you want to cast this object back to B to use member functions that only B provides, you need to use `dynamic_cast`.

A few things about `dynamic_cast`. First, it only works on pointer-to-pointer or reference-to-reference conversions. Second, it can't actually cast an object from an A to a B if the object is not, in fact, a B (or of a type derived from B). A pointer-to-pointer `dynamic_cast` that fails returns null. A reference-to-reference failure throws a `std::bad_cast` exception.

`reinterpret_cast`

The `reinterpret_cast` operator is a direct conversion with very few good uses. Most its operations give undefined results. What this means in practice is that you should read the compiler vendor's documentation before using it for anything.

One use for it, as we saw in **StorageDurationSample**, is to cast a pointer to an integer type large enough to hold it. This gives the memory address of the pointer, which can be useful for debugging and tracing operations where you can dump data to log files and create core dumps, but it may not be able to run a debugger easily. You will see it used legitimately at times for other purposes, but in general, it should be considered as the cast of last resort (excluding a C-style cast, which comes after `reinterpret_cast`).

C-style Cast

The C-style cast, (e.g., `auto someData = (SomeType)dataOfSomeOtherType;`) is not your friend. You are undoubtedly familiar with it from C#, where it is highly useful. In C#, if you try to make a cast using that syntax, and the cast is invalid, you will produce an InvalidCastException. This happens because the CLR keeps track of the types of everything you've created and detects bad casts.

C++ does not check to see if your C-style cast is valid, assuming it compiles, of course. C++ just assumes that it is. If it's a bad cast, and you are lucky, your program will crash immediately. If not, you will end up with data in an unknown state, which will certainly become corrupted in subtle and insidious ways.

Further, unlike the other casts, which you can easily spot by looking for `_cast<`, C-style casts do not stick out. When you're scanning lots of code quickly, parentheses wrapped around text looks as much like a function call as it does a cast operation. You could use a regular expression search for this in Visual Studio 2012: `\(.*\)[A-Za-z]`. Even so, you are still forgoing all the benefits and protections of the other casts.

The one thing a C-style cast can do that other casts cannot is cast an object to one of its protected or private inheritance base classes. You really shouldn't do this since, if you need public inheritance, you should use public inheritance.

In short, don't use C-style casts.

Sample

There is a sample, **CastingSample**, that demonstrates the many possible types of casting. It is included with the source code for this book. In the interest of brevity, I am omitting it here.

Chapter 9   Strings

Introduction

Strings are one of those troublesome things in C and C++. In the early days of the languages, strings were all character arrays, typically 7-bit ASCII (though perhaps EBCDIC on IBM mainframes that C was ported to). Then came a mess of OS-specific workarounds, such as code pages, to allow for languages with characters that were not in the English alphabet. After a period of chaos, came Unicode. Then Unicode. And then Unicode again. And a few more Unicodes here and there as well, which is the root of the problem today.

Unicode is, in essence, two things. It's a defined series of code points in which there is a one-to-one mapping of a particular code point to a particular value, some are graphic, others control and manipulate formatting or provide other required information. Everyone who uses Unicode agrees on all of these, including the private-use code points, which all agree are reserved for Unicode-conforming applications. So far, so good.

Then there are the encoding schemes where the divisions come from. There are 1,114,112 code points in Unicode. How do you represent them? The answer was the encoding schemes. UTF-16 was the first. It was later followed by UTF-8 and UTF-32. There are also endianness issues with some of these.

Other formats came and went, some of which were never even part of Unicode.

Windows ultimately adopted UTF-16 as did .NET and Java. Many GNU/Linux and other UNIX-like systems adopted UTF-8. Some UNIX-like systems use UTF-32. Some might use UTF-16. The web uses UTF-8 for the most part, due to that encoding's intentional design to be mostly backward compatible with ASCII. As long as you are working on one system, all is well. When you try to become cross-platform, things can become more confusing.

`char*` Strings

The `char*` strings (pointers to arrays of `char`) originally meant ASCII strings. Now they *sometimes* mean ASCII, but more frequently, they mean UTF-8. This is especially true in the UNIX world.

When programming for Windows, generally, you should assume that a `char*` string is an ASCII string or a code-page string. Code pages use the extra bit left over from 7-bit ASCII to add another 128 characters, thus creating a lot of localized text still fitting within one byte per character.

`wchar_t*` Strings

`wchar_t*` strings (pointers to arrays of `wchar_t`, also called *wide characters*) use a different, implementation-dependent character set. On Windows, this means a 16-bit value, which is used for UTF-16. You should always work with `wchar_t` as your native character type for Windows unless you have to support really, really old OS versions (i.e., the old Windows 9X series).

When you write a wide character string constant in code, you prefix the opening double quotes with an *L*. For example: `const wchar_t* s = L"Hello World";`. If you only need a single character, you again use the *L*, but with single quotes: `wchar_t ch = L'A';`.

`std::string` and `std::wstring` Strings

The `std::string` and `std::wstring` classes are found in the `<string>` header file. As you might imagine, `std::string` corresponds to `char*` while `std::wstring` corresponds to `wchar_t*`.

These classes provide a convenient way to store variable length strings and should be used for class member variables in place of their corresponding raw pointers (`char*` and `wchar_t*`). You should only use the raw pointers to pass strings as arguments, and then only if the string will be used as-is or copied locally into one of these string types.

In either case, the function should take in the string pointer as a pointer to `const` (e.g., `const wchar_t* someStr`). After all, pointers do not incur the same construction and destruction expense that `std::string` and `std::wstring` do. Using a pointer to `const` ensures that the function will not accidentally modify the data or try to free the memory that is pointed to.

To get a pointer to `const` for the contents of one of these, call its `c_str` member function. Note that the returned pointer points to `const` since the data should not be modified, nor should `delete` be called on the pointer. The memory is still owned and managed by the underlying `std::string` or `std::wstring` instance. This also means that if the underlying instance is destroyed, the pointer that `c_str` gives you becomes invalid, which is why, if you need the string data beyond the scope of the function it is being passed to, you should always store the string data in one of these types rather than storing the pointer directly.

To add text, use the `append` member function.

To see if a particular sequence of characters occurs in a string, use the `find` member function or one of its more specific variants, such as `find_first_of`. If the sequence is not in the string, then the return value will equal `std::npos`. Otherwise, it will be the index of the relevant starting point for the sequence.

To get a sub-string, use the `substr` member function, passing it the starting zero-based index and the number of elements (i.e. the number of `char` or `wchar_t` characters) to copy. It will return a `std::string` or a `std::wstring` without allowing you to overflow a buffer by passing an inaccurate count or an improper starting index.

There are other useful methods, all of which are documented as part of the basic_string class, which is a template class that `std::string` and `std::wstring` are predefined specializations of.

std::wstringstream Strings

The std::wstringstream class (there is a std::stringstream as well) is similar to the .NET StringBuilder class. It is usable in much the same way as any other C++ Standard Library stream. I find this type very useful for constructing a string within a member function that will then be stored in a std::wstring class member.

For an example of its usage, see the Toppings::GetString member function in the ConstructorsSample\Toppings.h file. Here is its code, just as a refresher:

```cpp
const wchar_t* GetString(void)
{
    if (m_toppings == None)
    {
        m_toppingsString = L"None";
        return m_toppingsString.c_str();
    }
    bool addSpace = false;
    std::wstringstream wstrstream;
    if (m_toppings & HotFudge)
    {
        if (addSpace)
        {
            wstrstream << L" ";
        }
        wstrstream << L"Hot Fudge";
        addSpace = true;
    }
    if (m_toppings & RaspberrySyrup)
    {
        if (addSpace)
        {
            wstrstream << L" ";
        }
        wstrstream << L"Raspberry Syrup";
        addSpace = true;
    }
```

```cpp
        if (m_toppings & CrushedWalnuts)
        {
            if (addSpace)
            {
                wstrstream << L" ";
            }
            wstrstream << L"Crushed Walnuts";
            addSpace = true;
        }
        if (m_toppings & WhippedCream)
        {
            if (addSpace)
            {
                wstrstream << L" ";
            }
            wstrstream << L"Whipped Cream";
            addSpace = true;
        }
        if (m_toppings & Cherry)
        {
            if (addSpace)
            {
                wstrstream << L" ";
            }
            wstrstream << L"Cherry";
            addSpace = true;
        }
        m_toppingsString = std::wstring(wstrstream.str());
        return m_toppingsString.c_str();
    }
```

Chapter 10 C++ Language Usages and Idioms

Overview

We've discussed the RAII idiom. Some language usages and programming idioms in C++ might seem foreign or pointless at first glance, but they do have a purpose. In this chapter, we will explore a few of these odd usages and idioms to understand where they came from and why they are used.

Incrementing and Decrementing

You will commonly see C++ increment an integer by using the syntax ++i instead of i++. The reason for this is partly historic, partly useful, and partly a sort of secret handshake. One of the common places you will see this is in a `for` loop (e.g., `for (int i = 0; i < someNumber; ++i) { ... }`). Why do C++ programmers use ++i rather than i++? Let's consider what these two operators mean.

```
int i = 0;

int x = ++i;

int y = i++;
```

In the previous code, when all three statements finish executing, i will be equal to 2. But what will x and y equal? They will both equal 1. This is because the pre-increment operator in the statement, ++i, means "increment i and give the new value of i as the result." So when assigning x its value, i goes from 0 to 1, and the new value of i, 1, is assigned to x. The post-increment operator in the statement i++ means "increment i and give the original value of i as the result." So when assigning y its value, i goes from 1 to 2, and the *original* value of i, 1, is assigned to y.

If we were to decompose that sequence of instructions step-by-step as written, eliminating the pre-increment and post-increment operators and replacing them with regular addition, we would realize that to perform the assignment to y, we need an extra variable to hold the original value of i. The result would be something like this:

```
int i = 0;

// int x = ++i;

i = i + 1;

int x = i;


// int y = i++;

int magicTemp = i;

i = i + 1;

int y = magicTemp;
```

Early compilers, in fact, used to do things like that. Modern compilers now determine that there are no observable side effects to assigning to y first, so the assembly code they generate, even without optimization, will typically look like the assembly-language equivalent of this C++ code:

```
int i = 0;
```

```
// int x = ++i;

i = i + 1;

int x = i;


// int y = i++;

int y = i;

i = i + 1;
```

In some ways, the ++i syntax (especially within a for loop) is a holdover from the early days of C++, and even C before it. Knowing that other C++ programmers use it, employing it yourself lets others know you have at least some familiarity with C++ usages and style—the secret handshake. The useful part is that you can write a single line of code, int x = ++i;, and get the result you desire rather than writing two lines of code: i++; followed by int x = i;.

Tip: While you can save a line of code here and there with tricks such as capturing the pre-increment operator's result, it's generally best to avoid combining a bunch of operations in a single line. The compiler isn't going to generate better code, since it will just decompose that line into its component parts (the same as if you had written multiple lines). Hence, the complier will generate machine code that performs each operation in an efficient manner, obeying the order of operations and other language constraints. All you'll do is confuse other people who have to look at your code. You'll also introduce a perfect situation for bugs, either because you misused something or because someone made a change without understanding the code. You'll also increase the likelihood that you yourself will not understand the code if you come back to it six months later.

Concerning Null – Use `nullptr`

At the beginning of its life, C++ adopted many things from C, including the usage of binary zero as the representation of a null value. This has created countless bugs over the years. I'm not blaming Kernighan, Ritchie, Stroustrup, or anyone else for this; it's amazing how much they accomplished when creating these languages given the computers available in the 70s and early 80s. Trying to figure out what things will be problems when creating a computer language is an extremely difficult task.

Nonetheless, early on, programmers realized that using a literal 0 in their code could produce confusion in some instances. For example, imagine you wrote:

```
int* p_x = p_d;



// More code here...


p_x = 0;
```

Did you mean to set the pointer to null as written (i.e. `p_x = 0;`) or did you mean to set the pointed-to value to 0 (i.e. `*p_x = 0;`)? Even with code of reasonable complexity, the debugger could take significant time to diagnose such errors.

The result of this realization was the adoption of the `NULL` preprocessor macro: `#define NULL 0`. This would help reduce errors, if you saw `*p_x = NULL;` or `p_x = 0;` then, assuming you and the other programmers were using the NULL macro consistently, the error would be easier to spot, fix, and the fix would be easier to verify.

But because the `NULL` macro is a preprocessor definition, the compiler would never see anything other than 0 due to textual substitution; it could not warn you about possibly erroneous code. If someone redefined the `NULL` macro to another value, all sorts of additional problems could result. Redefining `NULL` is a very bad thing to do, but sometimes programmers do bad things.

C++11 has added a new keyword, `nullptr`, which can and should be used in place of `0`, `NULL`, and anything else when you need to assign a null value to a pointer or check to see if a pointer is null. There are several good reasons to use it.

The `nullptr` keyword is a language keyword; it is not eliminated by the preprocessor. Since it passes through to the compiler, the compiler can detect errors and generate usage warnings that it couldn't detect or generate with the literal `0` or any macros.

It also cannot be redefined either accidentally or intentionally, unlike a macro such as `NULL`. This eliminates all the errors that macros can introduce.

Lastly, it provides future proofing. Having binary zero as the null value was a practical decision when it was made, but it was arbitrary nonetheless. Another reasonable choice might have been to have null be the max value of an unsigned native integer. There are positives and negatives to such a value, but there's nothing I know of that would have made it unusable.

With `nullptr`, it suddenly becomes feasible to change what null is for a particular operating environment without making changes to any C++ code that has fully adopted `nullptr`. The compiler can take a comparison with `nullptr`, or the assignment of `nullptr` to a pointer variable, and generate whatever machine code the target environment requires from it. Trying to do the same with a binary 0 would be very difficult, if not impossible. If in the future someone decides to design a computer architecture and operating system that adds a null flag bit for all memory addresses to designate null, modern C++ could support that because of `nullptr`.

Strange-Looking Boolean Equality Checks

You will commonly see people write code such as `if (nullptr == p_a) { ... }`. I have not followed that style in the samples because it simply looks wrong to me. In the 18 years I have been writing programs in C and C++, I have never had a problem with the issue this style avoids. Nonetheless, other people have had such problems. This style might possibly be part of the style rules you are required to follow; therefore, it is worth discussing.

If you wrote `if (p_a = nullptr) { ... }` instead of `if (p_a == nullptr) { ... }`, then your program would assign the null value to `p_a` and the `if` statement would always evaluate to false. C++, owing to its C heritage, allows you to have an expression that evaluates to any integral type within the parentheses of a control statement, such as `if`. C# requires that the result of any such expression be a Boolean value. Since you cannot assign a value to something like `nullptr` or to constant values, such as 3 and 0.0F, if you put that R-value on the left side of an equality check, the compiler will alert you to the error. This is because you would be assigning a value to something that cannot have a value assigned to it.

For this reason, some developers have taken up writing their equality checks this way. The important part is not which style you choose, but that you are aware that an assignment inside of something such as an `if` expression is valid in C++. That way, you know to look out for such problems.

Whatever you do, do not intentionally write statements like `if (x = 3) { ... }`. That is very bad style, which makes your code harder to understand and more prone to developing bugs.

throw() and noexcept(bool expression)

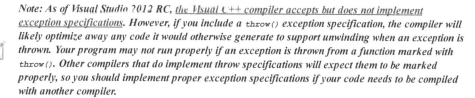

Note: As of Visual Studio 2012 RC, the Visual C++ compiler accepts but does not implement exception specifications. However, if you include a `throw()` exception specification, the compiler will likely optimize away any code it would otherwise generate to support unwinding when an exception is thrown. Your program may not run properly if an exception is thrown from a function marked with `throw()`. Other compilers that do implement throw specifications will expect them to be marked properly, so you should implement proper exception specifications if your code needs to be compiled with another compiler.

Note: Exception specifications using the `throw()` syntax (called dynamic-exception specifications) are deprecated as of C++11. As such, they may be removed from the language in the future. The `noexcept` specification and operator are replacements for this language feature but are not implemented in Visual C++ as of Visual Studio 2012 RC.

C++ functions can specify via the `throw()` exception specification keyword whether or not to throw exceptions, and if so, what kind to throw.

For example, `int AddTwoNumbers(int, int) throw();` declares a function that, due to the empty parentheses, states it does not throw any exceptions, excluding those it catches internally and does not re-throw. By contrast, `int AddTwoNumbers(int, int) throw(std::logic_error);` declares a function that states it can throw an exception of type `std::logic_error`, or any type derived from that.

The function declaration `int AddTwoNumber(int, int) throw(...);` declares that it can throw an exception of any type. This syntax is Microsoft-specific, so you should avoid it for code that may need to be compiled with something other than the Visual C++ compiler.

If no specifier appears, such as in `int AddTwoNumbers(int, int);`, then the function can throw any exception type. It is the equivalent of having the `throw(...)` specifier.

C++11 added the new `noexcept(bool expression)` specification and operator. Visual C++ does not support these as of Visual Studio 2012 RC, but we will discuss them briefly since they will undoubtedly be added in the future.

The specifier `noexcept(false)` is the equivalent of both `throw(...)` and of a function without a `throw` specifier. For example, `int AddTwoNumbers(int, int) noexcept(false);` is the equivalent of both `int AddTwoNumber(int, int) throw(...);` and `int AddTwoNumbers(int, int);`.

The specifiers `noexcept(true)` and `noexcept` are the equivalent of `throw()`. In other words, they all specify that the function does not allow any exceptions to escape from it.

When overriding a virtual member function, the exception specification of the override function in the derived class cannot specify exceptions beyond those declared for the type it is overriding. Let's look at an example.

```
#include <stdexcept>
```

```cpp
#include <exception>


class A
{
public:
    A(void) throw(...);
    virtual ~A(void) throw();

    virtual int Add(int, int) throw(std::overflow_error);
    virtual float Add(float, float) throw();
    virtual double Add(double, double) throw(int);
};


class B : public A
{
public:
    B(void); // Fine, since not having a throw is the same as throw(...).
    virtual ~B(void) throw(); // Fine since it matches ~A.

    // The int Add override is fine since you can always throw less in
    // an override than the base says it can throw.
    virtual int Add(int, int) throw() override;

    // The float Add override here is invalid because the A version says
    // it will not throw, but this override says it can throw an
    // std::exception.
    virtual float Add(float, float) throw(std::exception) override;

    // The double Add override here is invalid because the A version says
    // it can throw an int, but this override says it can throw a double,
    // which the A version does not specify.
    virtual double Add(double, double) throw(double) override;
};
```

Because the throw exception specification syntax is deprecated, you should only use the empty parentheses form of it, throw(), in order to specify that a particular function does not throw exceptions; otherwise, just leave it off. If you want to let others know what exceptions your functions can throw, consider using comments in your header files or in other documentation, making sure to keep them up-to-date.

`noexcept(bool expression)` is also an operator. When used as an operator, it takes an expression that will evaluate to *true* if it cannot throw an exception, or *false* if it can throw an exception. Note that the result is a simple evaluation; it checks to see if all functions called are `noexcept(true)`, and if there are any throw statements in the expression. If it finds any throw statements, even ones that you know are unreachable, (e.g., `if (x % 2 < 0) { throw "This computer is broken"; }`) it can, nonetheless, evaluate to *false* since the compiler is not required to do a deep-level analysis.

Pimpl (Pointer to Implementation)

The pointer-to-implementation idiom is an older technique that has been getting a lot of attention in C++. This is good, because it is quite useful. The essence of the technique is that in your header file you define your class' public interface. The only data member you have is a private pointer to a forward-declared class or structure (wrapped in a `std::unique_ptr` for exception-safe memory handling), which will serve as the actual implementation.

In your source code file, you define this implementation class and all of its member functions and member data. The public functions from the interface call into the implementation class for its functionality. The result is that once you've settled on the public interface for your class, the header file never changes. Thus, the source code files that include the header will not need to be recompiled due to implementation changes that do not affect the public interface.

Whenever you want to make changes to the implementation, the only thing that needs to be recompiled is the source code file where that implementation class exists, rather than every source code file that includes the class header file.

Here is a simple sample.

Sample: PimplSample\Sandwich.h

```
#pragma once

#include <memory>


class SandwichImpl;


class Sandwich
{
public:
        Sandwich(void);
        ~Sandwich(void);


        void AddIngredient(const wchar_t* ingredient);
        void RemoveIngredient(const wchar_t* ingredient);
        void SetBreadType(const wchar_t* breadType);
        const wchar_t* GetSandwich(void);


private:
```

```
    std::unique_ptr<SandwichImpl> m_pImpl;
};
```

Sample: PImplSample\Sandwich.cpp

```cpp
#include "Sandwich.h"
#include <vector>
#include <string>
#include <algorithm>

using namespace std;

// We can make any changes we want to the implementation class without
// triggering a recompile of other source files that include Sandwich.h since
// SandwichImpl is only defined in this source file. Thus, only this source
// file needs to be recompiled if we make changes to SandwichImpl.
class SandwichImpl
{
public:
    SandwichImpl();
    ~SandwichImpl();

    void AddIngredient(const wchar_t* ingredient);
    void RemoveIngredient(const wchar_t* ingredient);
    void SetBreadType(const wchar_t* breadType);

    const wchar_t* GetSandwich(void);

private:
    vector<wstring>           m_ingredients;
    wstring                   m_breadType;
    wstring                   m_description;
};

SandwichImpl::SandwichImpl()
{
}
```

```cpp
SandwichImpl::~SandwichImpl()
{
}


void SandwichImpl::AddIngredient(const wchar_t* ingredient)
{
    m_ingredients.emplace_back(ingredient);
}


void SandwichImpl::RemoveIngredient(const wchar_t* ingredient)
{
    auto it = find_if(m_ingredients.begin(), m_ingredients.end(), [=] (wstring item) -> bool
    {
        return (item.compare(ingredient) == 0);
    });

    if (it != m_ingredients.end())
    {
        m_ingredients.erase(it);
    }
}


void SandwichImpl::SetBreadType(const wchar_t* breadType)
{
    m_breadType = breadType;
}


const wchar_t* SandwichImpl::GetSandwich(void)
{
    m_description.clear();
    m_description.append(L"A ");
    for (auto ingredient : m_ingredients)
    {
        m_description.append(ingredient);
```

```cpp
        m_description.append(L", ");
    }

    m_description.erase(m_description.end() - 2, m_description.end());

    m_description.append(L" on ");

    m_description.append(m_breadType);

    m_description.append(L".");


    return m_description.c_str();
}


Sandwich::Sandwich(void)

    : m_pImpl(new SandwichImpl())

{

}


Sandwich::~Sandwich(void)

{

}


void Sandwich::AddIngredient(const wchar_t* ingredient)

{

    m_pImpl->AddIngredient(ingredient);

}


void Sandwich::RemoveIngredient(const wchar_t* ingredient)

{

    m_pImpl->RemoveIngredient(ingredient);

}


void Sandwich::SetBreadType(const wchar_t* breadType)

{

    m_pImpl->SetBreadType(breadType);

}


const wchar_t* Sandwich::GetSandwich(void)
```

```
{
        return m_pImpl->GetSandwich();
}
```

Sample: PimplSample\PimplSample.cpp

```cpp
#include <iostream>
#include <ostream>

#include "Sandwich.h"
#include "../pchar.h"

using namespace std;

int _pmain(int /*argc*/, _pchar* /*argv*/[])
{
    Sandwich s;
    s.AddIngredient(L"Turkey");
    s.AddIngredient(L"Cheddar");
    s.AddIngredient(L"Lettuce");
    s.AddIngredient(L"Tomato");
    s.AddIngredient(L"Mayo");
    s.RemoveIngredient(L"Cheddar");
    s.SetBreadType(L"a Roll");

    wcout << s.GetSandwich() << endl;

    return 0;
}
```

Chapter 11   Templates

Overview

Template functions and classes serve a similar purpose in C++ as generics serve in C#. They allow you to reuse your code without writing a function or class for each variant you want. As long as the types you supply to the template have the functionality associated with them that the template uses, all is well. If not, then the compiler will generate an error. This is because the compiler is generating a unique class for each specialization you use. Because the compiler builds classes and functions from your program's templates, template functions and classes must be put into header files and defined entirely inline. That way, the compiler can parse them for all source code files that use them.

Ultimately, templates can become very complex. The C++ Standard Library demonstrates the power and complexity of advanced templates. Despite that, you do not need an advanced knowledge of templates to use them effectively. An understanding of the fundamentals of C++ templates will help you unlock a significant amount of functionality and power.

Template Functions

A template function is a stand-alone function that takes at least one template argument. The fact that it takes an argument makes it incomplete until it is called with a concrete argument, thereby causing the template to become a fully defined function. Here is a template function that takes in two arguments.

Sample: TemplatesSample\PeekLastItem.h

```
#pragma once


template<class T, class U>

U PeekLastItem(T& collection)

{

    return *collection.rbegin();

}
```

The creation of any template—function or class—starts with the keyword `template` followed by the parameters within arrow brackets, as seen in the previous sample with `class T` and `class U`. The use of the word `class` before `T` and `U` does not mean those arguments must be classes. Think of `class` instead as a general word intended to convey the meaning of a non-specific type. You could have a template with concrete types or with a mixture of non-specific *class* types and concrete types, such as `template<class T, int>`. The use of `T` as the name for the first argument and `U` for a second is a common practice, not a requirement. You could use almost anything as a template argument name.

The previous function takes in a reference to an item of type T. It presumes that T will have a member function called `rbegin`, which can be called with no arguments and will return a pointer type that, when de-referenced, will become an object of type U. This particular function is designed primarily to work with many of the C++ Standard Library's collection classes, though any class that meets the assumptions the function makes about type T can be used with this template function. That ability to take any type, add the requisite functionality to it, and thereby make it eligible for use with a template is the main draw of templates.

Template Classes

Template classes are similar to template functions, only they are *classes* rather than simple stand-alone functions. Let's look at an example.

Sample: TemplatesSample\SimpleMath.h

```cpp
#pragma once

template<class T>

class SimpleMath
{
public:

    SimpleMath(void) { }

    ~SimpleMath(void) { }

    T Add(T a, T b)
    {
        return a + b;
    }

    T Subtract(T a, T b)
    {
        return a - b;
    }

    T Multiply(T a, T b)
    {
        return a * b;
    }

    T Divide(T a, T b)
    {
        return a / b;
    }
};
```

As the name implies, this class is not meant to be more than a demonstration. There is only one type argument. Looking at the class definition, we can deduce that the requirements for T in this case are that it has the following operators, all of which operate on two instances of T and return an instance of T:

- +
- -
- *
- /

While these logically belong with numbers, you can define these operators for any class or data type and then instantiate an instance of this template class, which is specialized for your custom class (e.g., a Matrix class).

One last note, if you were to define the member functions outside of the class definition, but still inside the same header file, of course, then you would need to use the inline keyword in the declarations; the definitions would look like this:

```
SimpleMath<T>::SimpleMath(void) { }.
```

This is the last file of this sample, showing a simple usage of each of the preceding templates.

Sample: TemplatesSample\TemplatesSample.cpp

```cpp
#include <iostream>

#include <ostream>

#include <vector>

#include "SimpleMath.h"

#include "PeekLastItem.h"

#include "../pchar.h"


using namespace std;


int _pmain(int /*argc*/, _pchar* /*argv*/[])

{

    SimpleMath<float> smf;


    wcout << "1.1F + 2.02F = " << smf.Add(1.1F, 2.02F) << "F." <<

        endl;


    vector<const wchar_t*> strs;
```

```cpp
    strs.push_back(L"Hello");

    strs.push_back(L"World");


    wcout << L"Last word was '" <<

        PeekLastItem<std::vector<const wchar_t*>,const wchar_t*>(strs) <<

        L"'." << endl;


    return 0;
}
```

Chapter 12   Lambda Expressions

No-Capture Lambdas

I assume that you have experience with lambdas from C#, so what we will do here is cover the syntax that C++ has adopted. All code snippets are from the same file in the same sample.

Sample: LambdaSample\LambdaSample.cpp

```
// Create a lambda-expression closure.

auto lm1 = []()

{

    wcout << L"No capture, parameterless lambda." << endl;

};


// Invoke the lambda.

lm1();
```

Lambdas with Parameters

```cpp
// Create a lambda closure with parameters.

auto lm2 = [](int a, int b)
{
    wcout << a << L" + " << b << " = " << (a + b) << endl;
};


lm2(3,4);
```

Specifying a Lambda's Return Type

The trailing return type here is -> `int` after the parameter specification.

```cpp
// Create a lambda closure with a trailing return type.
auto lm3 = [](int a, int b) -> int
{
    wcout << a << L" % " << b << " = ";
    return a % b;
};


wcout << lm3(7, 5) << endl;
```

Capturing Outside Variables

```
int a = 5;

int b = 6;

// Capture by copy all variables that are currently in the scope.

// Note also that we do not need to capture the closure;

// here we simply invoke the anonymous lambda with the

// () after the closing brace.

[=]()

{

    wcout << a << L" + " << b << " = " << (a + b) << endl;

    //// It's illegal to modify a here because we have

    //// captured by value and have not specified that

    //// this lambda should be treated as mutable.

    //a = 10;

}();


[=]() mutable -> void

{

    wcout << a << L" + " << b << " = " << (a + b) << endl;

    // By marking this lambda as mutable, we can now modify a.

    // Since we are capturing by value, the modifications

    // will not propagate outside.

    a = 10;

}();


wcout << L"The value of a is " << a << L"." << endl;


[&]()

{

    wcout << a << L" + " << b << " = " << (a + b) << endl;

    // By capturing by reference, we now do not need
// to mark this as mutable.

    // Because it is a reference, though, changes now

    // propagate out.
```

```cpp
        a = 10;
}();


wcout << L"The value of a is " << a << L"." << endl;

// Here we specify explicitly that we are capturing a by
// value and b as a reference.
[a,&b]()
{
    b = 12;
    wcout << a << L" + " << b << " = " << (a + b) << endl;
}();


// Here we specify explicitly that we are capturing b as
// a reference and that all other captures should be by
// value.
[=,&b]()
{
    b = 15;
    wcout << a << L" + " << b << " = " << (a + b) << endl;
}();


// Here we specify explicitly that we are capturing a by
// value and that all other captures should be by reference.
[&,a]()
{
    b = 18;
    wcout << a << L" + " << b << " = " << (a + b) << endl;
}();
```

Lambdas in Class-Member Functions

When you use a lambda in a class-member function, you cannot use a default capture by reference. This is because the lambda will be provided with a `this` pointer, and it must be copied. Also, when dealing with reference-counted smart pointers, it's common to run into problems with the lambda holding a reference to the class. Usually you will never get back to a reference count of zero, causing a memory leak in your program.

Chapter 13   C++ Standard Library

Introduction

There are far more things in the C++ Standard Library than we have time to cover. We will limit ourselves to looking at some of the most commonly used features that we haven't yet explored.

Iterators

Iterators serve the same purpose as IEnumerable and related interfaces in .NET, such as providing a common way to navigate through collections. Given a std::vector, for example, you can loop through its collection of items using the following code:

```
vector<int> vec;

vec.push_back(1);

vec.push_back(4);

vec.push_back(7);

vec.push_back(12);

vec.push_back(8);


for (auto i = begin(vec); i != end(vec); i++)

{

    wcout << *i << endl;

}
```

The std::begin function provides an iterator pointing to the first item of the collection. std::end provides an iterator that signals we have reached the end of a collection; the last item of the collection, assuming the collection has any items, is one item before the item we are given by std::end. That's why we check for != in the for loop. If no items are in the collection, then std::begin and std::end will return the same value.

In addition to the iterators from those two template functions, many collections provide const iterators via member functions named cbegin and cend, reverse iterators (that loop through a collection backwards) via rbegin and rend, and const reverse iterators via crbegin and crend. In the previous example, you can replace begin(vec) with vec.rbegin() and end(vec) with vec.rend() to go through the vector in reverse.

Range-Based `for` Loops

C++11 has added an additional type of `for` loop, called the range-based `for` loop, which provides functionality similar to the `foreach` loop in C#. The range-based `for` loop uses iterators and saves you the trouble of de-referencing pointers and the possibility of improperly checking for the end. The range-based `for` loop equivalent to the `for` loop in the previous example looks like this:

```
for (auto item : vec)

{

    wcout << item << endl;

}
```

`std::vector` and Other Containers

The collection you are likely to use most is `std::vector`. It is a fast, general-purpose collection similar to `List<T>` in .NET. It is found in the `<vector>` header file.

To add an item to the end of a vector, use the member function `push_back`. To remove an item from the end of a vector, use `pop_back`. You can access items at their index using `[]` the same way you would an array. To add an element or range of elements at a specific zero-based index, use the `insert` member function. To remove an element or range of elements at a specific zero-based index, use the `erase` member function.

A neat feature added in C++11 is the in-place construction functionality provided by the `emplace` and `emplace_back` member functions. Rather than constructing an object and then using `insert` or `push_back` to add it to the vector, you can call `emplace_back` and simply pass it the same arguments you would pass to the constructor for the type that the vector is holding. The vector will then construct and add a new instance of the object without the extra calculations that come with a copy or a move, and without using extra local memory.

The `emplace` function works the same, except you start by passing it an iterator that specifies the location. You can use `cbegin()` or `cend()` to add items to the beginning or end of the vector. If you have a specific zero-based index you want to emplace an item at, you can use `vec.cbegin() + idx`. You can also subtract from `cend()` if you want to place an item some number of spaces from the end.

`vector` offers more functionality, so you should definitely explore it further. The `at` member function will give you an item at an index, for example. There are ways to tell the vector to resize its internal capacity so you have more room free—if you knew you would need exactly 125 items, for instance—or so you minimize memory usage—if you added all the elements it will ever need and memory constraints are tight.

In addition to `std::vector`, several similar containers have different use cases. `std::vector` itself is the best choice when you need extremely fast, random access—when you will mostly be adding items to and removing items from the very end of the collection. If you also need to add items frequently to the front of the collection, you should consider using `std::deque` instead.

Use `std::queue` for a first-in, first-out container. Use `std::stack` for a last-in, first-out container.

The `std::map` class provides a sorted dictionary. `std::unordered_map` provides a hash table.

The `std::set` class is a sorted, keyed collection where the item stored is its own key, so each element must be unique. `std::unordered_set` is the unsorted equivalent of `std::set`.

The `std::list` class provides a doubly linked list. `std::forward_list` provides a singly linked list.

The `<algorithm>` Header

The `<algorithm>` header contains many very useful functions: things such as `find`, `sort`, `copy`, and all their related methods. The best way to learn them is to experiment with them.

The C Run-Time Library (CRT)

Some functionality from the C Runtime Library can be useful. Generally, the best way to access the library is to include the relevant `<c____>` header file, such as `<cstdlib>`.

Chapter 14   Visual Studio and C++

IntelliSense

If you're using almost any of the Visual Studio keyboard mappings, typing Ctrl+J will bring up IntelliSense. In Visual Studio 2012, IntelliSense should appear automatically in C++. In Visual Studio 2010 and earlier, you need to invoke it manually.

Code Snippets

Code snippets are a new feature for C++ in Visual Studio 2012. They did not exist in earlier versions. If you've never used them in any language, then in a C# project, start typing "for" to begin a `for` loop; once IntelliSense has chosen the `for` snippet, press the Tab key twice and watch as a `for` loop appears complete with automatic fields you can edit. Use the Tab key to switch between fields. When you're done editing the fields, press Enter. The cursor will be transported within the loop body with the field edits you made appearing as normal text.

Code snippets are particularly nice for switch statements that switch on an enum, since they will automatically populate the switch statement with all of the enum's members.

Including Libraries

In C++, it's usually not enough to just include a header file. Normally you need to tell the linker to link against a library that implements the code declared in the header file. To do this, you need to edit the project's properties, accessible in the **Project** menu as **ProjectName Properties…**

In the properties, under **Configuration Properties** > **Linker** > **Input**, one of the fields is **Additional Dependencies**. This is a semicolon-separated list of the **.LIB** files you need to link against. It should end with `%(AdditionalDependencies)` so that any additional libraries linked via MS Build will be added.

For a typical DirectX 11 Metro-style game, for example, you might see the following:

d2d1.lib; d3d11.lib; dxgi.lib; ole32.lib; windowscodecs.lib; dwrite.lib; xaudio2.lib; xinput.lib; mfcore.lib; mfplat.lib; mfreadwrite.lib; mfuuid.lib; %(AdditionalDependencies)

If you receive a linker error telling you it cannot find a definition of something you are using, find the function or class on MSDN; the documentation will tell you both the header file and the library file you need.

Generating Assembly Code Files

If you want to view a very close approximation of the assembly code that your code is compiled into, in your project's properties, under **Configuration Properties** > **C/C++** > **Output Files**, set the **Assembler Output** option to something other than **No Listing**.

I'd recommend either **Assembly-Only Listing (/FA)** or **Assembly with Source Code (/FAs)**. **Assembly-Only Listing** sprinkles enough line-number comments that you can usually cross-reference with your source code files to see what C++ code corresponds with the assembly code. That can be helpful if you want one place to see everything rather than flipping back and forth between whatever you've opened the .ASM file in (I use Notepad++) and Visual Studio.

Note that the generated assembly uses MASM macros (find them on MSDN). If you don't know what a particular assembly instruction means (e.g., LEA), you can search the internet for it or download the appropriate programming manual from Intel's site (assuming x86/Itanium), AMD's site (assuming x64) or ARM Holding's site (assuming ARM). If you've never learned any assembly, I definitely recommend doing so (try creating a simple Windows Console app).

Understanding assembly gives you a better understanding of how computers really work internally. Combine that with the knowledge that computers are all hardwired to begin executing the same code every time they are powered on (traditionally the BIOS on PCs, though that is now being replaced by UEFI), and the mystery of how and why computers work quickly begins to fade.